Look Up

Look Up

FIVE PRINCIPLES FOR INTENTIONAL LEADERSHIP

Carolyn Chism Hardy

"What is lacking is acknowledgment of the need for everyday advice. Respect your elders by learning from their life experiences."

— Lois Henderson Chism

Contents

Dedication........i
Forward.........vii

Introduction..1

1. Plan Your Destiny...................................5

Know Your Why   13

Balance   19

Don't Eat Excuses for Breakfast   26

2. Make the Right Impression..............32

Know Your Worth   38

Stand Out   44

Don't Let Bad News Age   51

3. Build Relationships **58**

Understand Personalities   63

Don't Leave Dead Bodies   71

Never Let a Good Problem Go to Waste   77

4. Be the Change You Wish to See..........................**83**

Use Your Education, Lean on Common Sense   90

Be Transparent   98

Become the Pro   106

5. Keep Calm and Carry On..................................**113**

Be Prepared   120

Lead by Example   128

Always Pursue Growth   134

Acknowledgments..**139**

Look Up

CAROLYN CHISM HARDY

Dedication

History is threaded with stories of inspiring women who have paved the way for future generations. Harriet Tubman, Rosa Parks, Maya Angelou, Ida B. Wells, Sojourner Truth and Mary McLeod Bethune inspired other women to accomplish great things.

These women are not remembered just for what they did. These women took action. And every action has a reaction. Each woman is remembered because of what she caused—a ripple effect that continues today.

They are honored with proclamations or bronze statues in city parks all over the world. We read about them in history books and study their incredible impact on the progression of civil rights, the importance of their creations and the glass ceilings they shattered along the way. But there is one woman whose impact on the world has not been stitched into the fabric of our narrative. Her name is not one you'll recognize, but her achievements are no less historic. You should remember her name. It might be one of the most remarkable names you'll ever hear. Let me tell you why.

Lois Henderson Chism was born in 1924 to share-croppers on a farm in Mississippi. Sharecroppers borrowed funds from landowners, so they could support their families and work the land. After every harvest, they had to pay the landlord back the loan. The system never allowed them to get ahead. She watched her parents struggle and wanted something different for her life.

As Lois grew up, she dreamed of earning a college education, starting a career and raising a family. But because of the way things were back then, she only completed the 11th grade. She married at the age of 18 and had 16 children over the next 24 years.

Society might say her legacy should have been a life of poverty for her children—and maybe even her grandchildren. The system she was born into was designed to oppress blacks. The world might tell you her kids would grow up to be broken.

But society can be so wrong because Lois Henderson Chism had other plans.

Dreaming gave her hope and saved her life. Her aspirations also fueled her spirit and nurtured the ability to inspire her children to dream as she did. She was their greatest mentor—and she knew it. So she went to work. While dreaming of a career, she read about powerful men and women. She studied the secrets to their success in corporate America, and she knew education was incredibly vital.

Lois painstakingly developed a plan to educate her flock. She started by encouraging her children to look beyond their circumstances. With 14 children underfoot—two passed away as babies—she taught, nurtured, loved and motivated them to accomplish what many never people never will.

Lois placed her life on "center stage" to teach her children the rules of life and what mistakes to avoid. She encouraged her children to seek higher education to gain the advantage of knowledge.

At the age of 44, Lois watched her first child receive a Bachelor of Science degree. Her dream of a better life for her children had come true. After that first degree, Lois managed, planned, supported and inspired

20 more Bachelor of Science degrees, 20 Master's Degrees, three doctorates and eight technical degrees, with 30 more currently in the making. She achieved her own dreams by teaching her children to become leaders.

Her reach wasn't limited to helping her children earn degrees. Her legacy goes beyond education. She has inspired and supported many great careers, such as CEOs, presidents, doctors, school principals, police majors, teachers, logistics professionals and business owners. Her children grew up to live and prosper in the prominent neighborhoods, where their parents and grandparents were formerly servants.

Even though she left school in the 11th grade—a choice that would have stopped many from achieving their dream—she saw it as a bump in the road rather than a closed door. She merely made an adjustment to her dream. She had the wisdom to change the world through others.

As you may have guessed, Lois Henderson Chism is my mother.

Her dream is the foundation of many key accomplishments in our family, with the most significant being my ownership of the largest black-owned brewery and bottling company in the world. Her sacrifices were not in vain. She gave her children everything so our dreams could be realized.

What was mom's secret? She was smart, had a business mindset and possessed the highest integrity. She was a psychologist without the degrees. She was an excellent planner and visionary. She will always be my first and greatest leader.

My mom was always there for me and always knew how to handle any situation. I remember my first business trip at the age of 20. I had never eaten at a white tablecloth restaurant. I said, "Mom what do I do?" She said, "Sit in the middle, watch everyone else and then order last!" Mom, thank you for your common sense, wisdom and all of your sacrifices. When I grow up, I want to be as smart as my mom. I'm not there yet, but I'm still trying!

My mother had the tenacity of Sojourner Truth, the fortitude of Harriett Tubman, the compassion of Maya Angelou, the courage of Rosa Parks, the empathy of Ida B. Wells and she had the business mind of Mary McLeod Bethune.

She was the best parts of these women and more. Each of them created an ever-lasting effect. My mother did the same. She will be remembered for more than what she did. It's what she caused that has become her legacy. She inspired the success of a new generation.

I'm a part of that legacy and so are my children. And their children will be, too. She lived a courageous life and motivated her 14 children who lived to adulthood to dream big. She held a torch, which lit a fire in us that continues to burn today. Because she dared to dream bigger than the world said she should, my siblings and I are leaving an impact on the world. Our children will continue to hold the torch that will light the way for generations to come.

This book is dedicated to my mother, Lois Henderson Chism. Without her, the words on these pages would not have been lived.

Thank you, mom, for all your sacrifices. I can see your light burning brighter than ever!

Thank you for your love, support and guidance.

Foreward
By Staley Cates

Great leaders fuel success, breakthroughs, innovation and cures. They come in all shapes and sizes. Some lead countries or armies, while others lead families. Every industry has great leaders. You find them in medicine, mathematics, fashion, sports and commerce. If you are looking to lead it helps to learn from those who have gone before you. If you have a chance to learn from one of the greats, you should seize it.

This book is your chance. Within these pages, you'll find the story of someone who truly embodies the spirit of leadership. Carolyn Chism Hardy is a leader of leaders. She has become a true luminary in any field she explores and has all the traits you look for in a leader.

Leaders have a vision. Helen Keller said, "The only thing worse than being blind is having sight but no vision." Carolyn grew up poor. It was the only thing she knew by the time she got to college. It's certainly not where she stayed. Carolyn knew from a very young age she was going to be successful because she had a vision for her future.

Leaders are strategic. Sun Tzu said, "Strategy without tactics is the slowest route to victory. Tactics without strategy is the noise before defeat." Carolyn knows how to create a plan and execute it flawlessly. Her ability to do this is possible because of her ability to adapt. When she comes up against a roadblock, she finds a way to go around. She is a pro at both tactics and strategy.

Leaders motivate. Winston Churchill said, "The Pessimist sees difficulty in every opportunity. The optimist sees opportunity in every difficulty." Carolyn motivates by example. She faces a challenge by looking for the opportunity. She teaches others to do the same. Great leaders motivate individuals to do more than they thought they were capable of doing. Carolyn perfected this time and again when she was hired to lead problem teams. She took departments that ranked dead last in the company and led them to be number one.

Leaders have integrity. Former First Lady Michelle Obama said, "We learned about honesty and integrity —that the truth matters...that you don't take shortcuts or play by your own set of rules...and success doesn't count unless you earn it fair and square. Carolyn has earned every bit of the success she has known. Her saying, "Transparency is the cousin of honesty" sums up her approach to handling problems and instilling trust with others.

Leaders are trailblazers. Albert Einstein said, "The person who follows the crowd will usually go no further than the crowd. The person who walks alone is likely to find himself in places no one has ever seen before." Carolyn was determined to change the status quo. She was the first African-American female in several different positions during her career. She knew she was breaking glass ceilings and felt she had a responsibility to those who would come after her. Carolyn did not take that responsibility lightly. She paved the way for others.

There are many key characteristics of great leaders. You will find direction on them in Carolyn's stories. You will learn how to emulate them with her direction. Carolyn has broken down her strategy into bite-size pieces that are easy for any reader to swallow. No matter where you are on your leadership journey this book is a guide to help you become a better leader. The principles are simple, but the direction is invaluable.

I hope you enjoy this book and learn a lot along the way. So, turn the page and start your journey to becoming a great leader. Best of luck and lots of learning.

Introduction

Notes are my companions. I write them all the time. When I have something I want to research further, I hear an interesting quote or I have an idea for a new business deal, I open my notepad and start writing. Over the years, I have filled thousands of pages with lessons learned and great ideas. Although I graduated from college years ago, these notes are a record of my continued education. I have been on a lifelong odyssey of growth and discovery. This book is a peek into my journey.

There is inherent value in learning from the path another has taken. These notes are the foundation for the guidance offered in this book. You hold in your hands a collection of golden nuggets of knowledge I learned along the way. Many were taught to me by mentors like my mother; Dick Jirsa, former CFO of Smucker's; Bob Morrison, the COO of Smucker's; and countless others. I learned many other lessons the hard way through trial and error.

Leaders are like lighthouses. They are aware people look up to them for guidance. They light the way so others may reach their destination safely. Leaders offer guidance to buffer those who come after them. They keep them from hitting the rocks that are surely on their paths. They stand firm in their position and confident in their actions. This book will help you navigate away from the rocks and steer you into calmer waters.

Many people choose to ignore great advice. Some want to figure things out on their own. It's a lonely road for those who believe they don't need help. Those who can't master the principles in this book may never reach their destination.

During my career, discrimination towards my race and gender was commonplace. I had to endure prejudices that were unjust and unfair, while maintaining my composure and work ethic. Overcoming obstacles that seemed insurmountable was critical to my success. I persevered because others who went before me showed me it was possible.

Our accomplishments as a society are many. I have witnessed others do things most never thought possible. I have watched as stereotypes and dated ideals have been crushed.

In my lifetime, I have seen African-Americans dominate both tennis and golf.

I watched the first female become the Speaker of the House of Representatives.

I even saw the swearing in of the country's first black President.

I'm proud a woman was finally awarded the Nobel Prize for Economics in 2009. As of press time, Elinor Ostrom is still the only female to receive this honor.

Every person can choose to see hope, courage and motivation in the stories of others. You can forge a path into uncharted territory if you learn the skills within these pages. Perhaps one day it will be your name listed as one of the "first" in some monumental category.

A great leader knows someone is always looking to them to be a role model, to motivate and lead the way. A French philosopher, Bernard of Chartres, once said,

"We stand on the shoulders of giants." Almost 900 years later, his words still stand true. I stood on the shoulders of my mother. She passed along her wisdom and enabled me to benefit from the life she lived. I hope to do the same for you.

I hope anyone interested in rising to the challenge of leadership or entrepreneurialism will find guidance in the lessons I learned and the notes I took along the way. Read this book, master the principles and remember to always "Look Up." You are one of the giants on which the future depends.

X

Plan Your Destiny

Have you ever been hungry? I'm not talking about the kind of hunger that comes from skipping a meal because you are too busy to eat. I mean famished. Have you ever been so hungry your body has gone long past stomach grumblings into pain only nourishment can quiet down? I have.

Sometimes when you have no food, the only thing you have to live on is your dreams. My mother may not have had much, but she knew how to feed our souls. She encouraged us to fill our minds with knowledge when our stomachs were empty. And above all, she inspired us to have a plan.

Hunger pangs aren't limited to your body. There are pangs that will haunt you when you have no direction.

If you hunger for more out of your life, you can experience a different kind of longing. But you will find it painful just the same.

I grew up in many impoverished neighborhoods throughout Memphis, Tenn. I lived in 13 different homes before I turned 12. None of them were larger than two bedrooms. There were 16 of us back then, all crammed into whatever tiny house my father found. Occasionally, he would move us without any warning. Usually, it was because he had not paid the rent and we had been evicted.

On summer days, I took my six younger siblings to the park to play. We would arrive in the morning and hang out until noon. That's when the park commission served lunch each day. The meal consisted of a sandwich with peanut butter or lunchmeat, an apple and something to drink. We depended upon that meal because food was so scarce. We always waited to see if they had extras, hoping we could take some home to our baby siblings. These little things in life were important to our survival. We were poor but happy.

At home, we were lucky to get a smidge of the worst peanut butter you ever tasted. It was called Big

Chief, and it was awful. My mother worked wonders with what she had and never complained. She didn't have time for it. Her time was spent helping us plan our future. We didn't have much, but we had each other.

When I was four-years-old, my mother would send me to the store to buy food. I would calculate the cost in my head to ensure the change was correct. It's no surprise I went to college to become a CPA. I think my mom did that on purpose.

As I was growing up, I watched my mom stretch a dollar and somehow manage to still save a little. She knew it was essential to save for the future, even if it was pennies at a time. I grew up learning to appreciate the little things, while planning for my big dreams.

My mother taught us to dream big. She had a plan for her girls to graduate from college and her sons to attend trade school. She used all the older sibling as our role models.

Based upon her plan, my oldest sister graduated from college and became a teacher. In my mind, her education immediately raised her out of poverty.

My eldest brother graduated from vocational school, started a career and was immediately raised out of poverty. Their transformation amazed us. As a child, the people we admired most in the world were our siblings, Juanita and Scnear. My mother required the older siblings to tutor the younger siblings. Mom used the idea of "train the trainer" before the business world embraced it. As a result, we all studied and prepared for college throughout high school.

One day when I was 16, my sister Debra and I went on an adventure. We drove my mother to a local high school where she worked as a custodian. As a rule, we were supposed to go straight home. My dad always wanted his car returned immediately. On this particular day, we decided to head in a different direction. We drove to the suburbs. The streets were lined with tall, beautiful trees. The houses were big, much larger than the homes in my neighborhood. Many were thousands of square feet larger than the two-bedroom home where we lived. The yards were big and perfectly manicured.

It was my first time driving in the area, and I had never seen such grandeur. Gazing out the window as the luxury passed by, I turned to my sister. "Debra, I'm going to live here one day," I said. She smiled and teased, "You are always dreaming."

I understand why it seemed silly to make such a declaration. I was a young girl living in unimaginable poverty. We were driving through a neighborhood where my relatives worked as servants. You could fit five houses like mine into one of the houses on this street. But I had a plan.

Within 10 years, I graduated from Memphis State, was hired as a staff accountant, passed the CPA exam and at the age of 26 moved to one of the nicest neighborhoods in the area. My husband and I bought a new home down the street from the one I dreamed about.

My siblings and I were all motivated to pursue higher education. My mother's six girls earned college degrees and her sons completed trade school. Mom's educational plan was a success.

A goal without a plan is only a wish. Therefore, the first step requires you to develop a plan. It must be specific and measurable.

I had to create one to pass the CPA exam. The plan had to balance my 60-hour workweek with the hours needed to study for the exam. To make this happen, I had to be the architect of my life, since I must live with the outcome.

I knew that schedule would not change just because I had an excellent plan to pass the CPA exam. I also knew that I had to balance my current job duties with my future plans. My company wasn't willing to grant paid leave, and I could not afford unpaid leave. I knew which areas of accounting were my strengths and which areas were my weaknesses. Additionally, I asked my mentors to discuss my strengths and weaknesses with brutal honesty.

My annual performance reviews were an excellent source of information. They listed my strengths as having integrity, selflessness, being dependable, detail oriented, aggressive, ambitious, driven, willing to make sacrifices and take risks. My weaknesses included being driven to win and working too hard. This constructive advice was vital to reworking my plan in the areas I needed to improve.

I gave myself a year and a half to pass the CPA exam. My strategy was to tackle two sections at a time, starting with the parts that were my strengths. Auditing was last on the list because I had little to no experience in this area. It worked, and I passed the exam as planned in a year and a half.

If you fail to plan, then you plan to fail. When you set goals and make your life a priority, you are motivated to approach execution with passion and energy. In executing a strategy for your personal development, clearly articulate who you are by outlining your strengths and weaknesses. Be bold and invest in your future by implementing your plan. You must take action. Never let anyone dictate your future or own who you'll become.

I took control of my education, created my professional development program and took advantage of every training opportunity offered. My company's tuition reimbursement benefit would fund my journey. I seized on the opportunity to better my education.

If you think you're capable of achieving more, turn in a different direction. You'll discover a new destiny waiting for you.

Check with your company to see if they offer tuition reimbursement. If yes, take advantage of it. According to a study funded by the Lumina Foundation, only 5 percent of employees participate in available programs. Continuing education must be an integral part of your plan.

I was young when I started planning for my future. But you are never too young to start and never too old to learn. Remember, destiny is a matter of choice, not a matter of chance.

At some point, you'll realize one of two things: Either you planned for your future or you didn't. What will you choose? Just remember, your future starts right now.

Know Your Why

As a teenager, I was entrusted with maximizing the family's weekly grocery budget. Each week, I shopped at the butcher, bakery and grocery store. I looked for the best prices at every stop and would only buy if the price was right. I was good with numbers and negotiations.

When I was 13 years old, my brother gave us an allowance to do chores. His goal was to get us to do more housework. I was motivated to earn money, so I subcontracted my chores at 50 percent of my earnings to my siblings, so I could spend my time reading.

As I was preparing to start college, mom asked if I planned to be a teacher like my older sister. I tutored my little brother, Maurice, for many years. After imagining a classroom with 30 kids like my little brother, I told her absolutely not. I was going straight to the business building. I planned to get as far away from teaching as possible by becoming a businesswoman.

After college, I started my first job as a staff accountant. I was 20 years old and straight out of poverty. The business world was utterly foreign to me, and the odds were stacked against me. I had no idea I would spend 25 years working for Smucker's. Additionally, I had no idea how hard it would be to leave.

After a quarter of a century with Smucker's, I decided my career with them was over. It was time to move on. This decision was tough and incredibly emotional. I cried going to interviews. I cried writing my goodbye speech. During my going-away party, I cried with my employees while delivering my goodbye speech. I had formed an emotional attachment that at times wasn't healthy for my career. I often put the company's needs ahead of my own. Many times, I was more loyal to them than I was to myself.

As I matured and assessed my impact, I realized I had more potential than this company could harness. But my love and loyalty were holding me back. I asked myself, "Why am I still here?" When I couldn't answer that simple question, I knew it was time to move on.

The decision to leave didn't minimize the impact Smucker's had on my career. When they hired me, no one knew where the job would lead. I came to them with a dream of a successful career and became loyal to the company's mission and culture. My loyalty was well placed since this company offered valuable experience in many disciplines. They provided mentors who supported my development. They provided tuition reimbursement for both my CPA license and master's degree. They appreciated and promoted me until I reached a glass ceiling.

There is a time and place for everything. My first job helped me become an exceptional leader. Being there for so long allowed me to recognize God's gifts. But to reach my full potential, I needed new experiences and opportunities outside of Smucker's.

After I announced I was leaving and would not change my mind, Smucker's invested in preparing me for my next opportunity. They hired a career consultant to objectively evaluate my skills for my desired career change. The assessment was a full day at an agency in

Nashville, Tenn. After eight hours, I met with the counselor to receive feedback. They said I was unusual. My profile revealed I could perform successfully in most careers. My next step was to understand my why.

When I walked through the doors of Smucker's for the first time, my "why" was to start my career as a businesswoman. Additionally, my "why" was to work for a company that would offer me a fair opportunity and show appreciation when I delivered.

So, I had to reconcile why I wanted to leave. The next step in my journey had to fill a void that Smucker's could not. I wanted to grow and achieve more. I needed to continue the climb. I was looking up at the possibilities a new position could offer. Knowing my purpose enabled me to turn down opportunities that didn't fit my personal growth plan. Understanding why I was jumping ship allowed me to look for the right boat to pick me up. By knowing my why, I landed a great opportunity at Coors Brewing Company.

When I started my new job, I knew there were still mountains to climb. At Smucker's, I was in the good ol' boys club. But I wanted to create my own club. I knew there were more accomplishments in my life. I knew I could shatter the glass ceilings, for myself and others, if I continued to focus on my why. My faith and belief in myself allowed me to continue my journey.

An essential step in the process is to check yourself on a regular basis. Why are you doing what you are doing? Do you feel full or is your soul feeling hungry? Is it grumbling for more? If you take the time to plan your destiny, it's critical to know why you want to head in the new direction. Knowing your why will allow you to adjust your plan if your purpose isn't being realized.

I had a supervisor who struggled with managing his team. Leadership was a chore for him. He was uncomfortable giving directions or providing performance feedback. He worked hard to avoid employee conflict and interactions. One day, I asked him about his future goals. He said he wanted to be a lawyer. However, with two children and a wife, meeting financial obligations was his priority. He was miserable as a supervisor and was close to being terminated.

I called a friend to see if he would interview the employee for a second-shift job. Then, we offered him a separation package sufficient to allow him to return to school. He got the job and changed his future. If you know your purpose, you can find creative ways to achieve your why.

Another growth strategy is to seek new opportunities with your current employer. This can occur through additional training, a promotion or lateral move. This may require you to assume new roles and responsibilities. Seek opportunities to stretch your capabilities, while gaining recognition for your contributions. Also, seek out mentors to help you strengthen areas of weakness. But always know why you need a change.

It is critical to know where you want to go in life. It is even more critical to understand why you want to go there. Having a purpose is the fuel you need to get further down the road when you run out of motivation. You have heard the expression, "Keep your eyes on the prize." Your why is the prize your life deserves.

X

Balance

My mother didn't attend her oldest children's graduation from high school because she had nothing to wear. There was never enough money for both her and the children. So she made the selfless choice and purchased clothes for the children who were graduating. Each of us understood the family's financial circumstances, and mom's internal struggles and pain. My older siblings comforted my mother by reassuring her that her absence wasn't a reflection of her commitment. They wouldn't push her to go because they wouldn't want her to be uncomfortable. They said they would make her proud.

Mom was our biggest cheerleader and teacher. She celebrated our unique accomplishments and kept awards and certificates that we had long ago forgotten. Mom never forgot. At every opportunity, she reminded us how proud she was of our accomplishments. She showed us our life could be different from hers. She challenged us to make better choices about education. She taught us about sacrificing, planning, passion and perseverance. If we could master these things, we would enjoy a different outcome. Mom had a fantastic ability to cope in situations where others would feel imbalanced. But she had the vision and the wisdom to teach us how to achieve balance.

Balance is one of the toughest pursuits of most professionals. How do you juggle family, work, friends and self? These are all important but not always equally important. There is no perfect, one-size fits all approach. Your individual work-life strategy must adapt over time, often on a daily basis. As you grow, and circumstances change, the way you balance your life will need to change. Balance in your life is like a fingerprint. It is unique to you.

As I climbed the corporate ladder, my mother was the primary caregiver when my children were sick. My mother taught us that women in corporate America were at a disadvantage. She said males, who make most promotional recommendations, would label women as "unreliable" if they missed work due to the responsibilities that come with raising a child. I never missed work because my children were sick. Our careers were so important to mom that some days she would not know the kids were coming until they arrived. During these visits, all grandchildren felt that sickness was a gift. They were blessed with an opportunity to spend the day with grandmother, "The Healer." She produced home remedies that always seemed to work and was never too busy for anyone. She loved to say, "Time with loved ones is more precious than gold." She taught us that family support is critical to maintaining balance.

Like many, I learned my lesson the hard way. As a young, professional, my career was all-consuming. My dedication to my job caused me to make a decision that changed my life. Nearly 20 years later, I still remember the emotional fallout from not finding the right balance in my life.

On the day of a loved one's funeral, I was coordinating an annual business function. The company never stated I couldn't attend the funeral. However, I chose to prioritize a business function over family. After missing the service, my heart would not allow me to find solace in my decision. I was sad. Guilt began to weigh heavy once reality set in. Work obligations were a poor excuse for not supporting my family in their time of grief. I couldn't shake the regret.

When your heart tells you something, you better listen. The lesson you learn might change your life. From that moment forward, I vowed I would never let work interfere with important family events. I knew the balance I needed was one that would allow me to sleep well at night when reflecting on the choices I made during the day. There were times when work would need to come first, perhaps causing me to miss an event at the school for one of my children. I consistently maintained a grasp on which obligations should be prioritized.

Obviously, my mother raised me better, but life has a way of awakening us. As a result, I demonstrated to my children that family is a priority. They understood work, friends and other distractions could pull you in multiple directions. There are times when you can't stay for the full event, but an effort must be made. When my mother passed away, all of her grandchildren flew from every part of the world to say goodbye. During her homecoming, they each said there was nothing in this world more important to them.

Marriage is not a competitive sport but a partnership. Balance is a challenge for two type-A personalities trained to succeed, especially with egos that may need to dominate or always be right. Typically, problems in relationships occur due to lack of communication and balance. Jealousy and ingratitude will end a partnership. The ideal mate is proud of you for achieving your personal best.

I met my husband, Marino, in college. We matured together, while continuing our education and starting our careers. We respect each other's differences by uplifting our strengths, while working together to improve our weaknesses. Effective communication was critical to balancing our complex life. If either of us had a business trip, we advised each other in advance. If we had a difficult week requiring minimum interruptions, the kids knew to call the other parent.

Balance was never an issue, since the family understood we were a two-career household. On occasion, the kids went to work with us. They enjoyed these times because they were proud of us. We modeled our ability to balance for our children.

My children were exposed to my balancing act at an early age. They never complained because they understood the necessity and sacrifice. They were always proud of our presence at their events. They knew at least one parent would attend. They took responsibility for reminding us of their activities. Jennifer, my oldest daughter, always made sure to make accommodations for my attendance.

I remember her induction into the National Honor Society. When leaving for an appointment, an urgent business problem would often arise causing some type of delay. Jennifer knew I typically ran late, so she placed a chair at the back of the room to allow me to arrive without embarrassment.

As usual, she heard the familiar tap of my heels as I walked through the door. She looked at me with pride in her eyes and a big smile on her face. My presence was more important than being on time.

Days like these serve as a reminder of why I continue my pursuit of balance. Murphy's law says, "If something can go wrong, it will." I now account for the unexpected in my schedule.

Our priorities will change as we enter different chapters of our lives. We must rebalance as we evolve. Heart, logic, achievement and enjoyment is always considered when I strive for balance. Through delegation, outsourcing and the elimination of activities that don't add value, I spend time on what matters and forget the rest. There are no do-overs.

We only get one life. Make it count.

X

Don't Eat Excuses for Breakfast

When I was a child, we ate a lot of rice. It was an inexpensive way to feed a large family. For some, it might be hard to believe there were times when we couldn't afford rice. Fortunately, necessity gave birth to creativity. My mother realized that she could not feed and nourish her children's bodies with excuses.

She could have easily blamed my father for not bringing home the money he promised, but the solution-oriented woman recognized the futility. Instead, she would provide by secretly saving some of the money my father brought home in weeks prior. She would buy a bag of onions for a nickel and work a miracle with a little flour. She understood that you couldn't eat excuses.

It is nearly impossible to make excuses when you are busy finding solutions. When you hide behind the temporary safety of an excuse, your growth stagnates. Accountability and responsibility are the facilitators of growth. Usually, responsibility is given to an individual to achieve the vision and goals of an organization. Accountability, however, is a choice to accept or reject the assigned responsibility.

Greater responsibility, autonomy, and control are typically granted to those who have proven themselves accountable on smaller tasks. They have demonstrated an understanding of the full scope of their job within the big picture. People who make excuses are typically passed over for promotions. Excuses also prevent them from garnering greater responsibilities and higher salaries associated with those promotions.

Leaders do not eat excuses for breakfast! If you are unable to master this principle, you may never become a successful leader. Each day is an opportunity for you to awaken and take control.

If you have handed power over to someone else by blaming them for what is going on in your life, it's time to take it back. Leaders recognize that organizational growth depends on their ability to address challenges. Excuses limit this progress.

There is nothing external that can truly limit you from living the life you deserve. Your motivation to achieve is an internal process fueled by purpose and your "why." Internal roadblocks can manifest as anxiety, lack of self-confidence, or hesitancy, and the only person who can give power to this hurdle is you. Addressing these mental obstacles is rarely easy, but making a change is 100 percent possible.

For example, someone is unhappy with their weight, and they travel frequently. This person often says they don't have time to exercise or eat healthy foods because they travel.

In reality, traveling isn't the reason for their weight issue. There is no direct cause-and-effect relationship between traveling and weight gain. The truth is this person has a weight issue due to poor dietary choices and limited physical activity. They are convinced traveling and the job are the limiting factors. This situation is perceived as hopeless. If weight loss was important, would ten minutes of exercise in a hotel room or taking the stairs instead of the elevator have been a consideration?

If this person would stop making excuses and create a plan, the change would be possible.

A can-do attitude is the first step in any journey. Henry Ford said, "Whether you think you can or you think you can't, you're right." So, what do you think? How do you spend most of your time: Making excuses or creating solutions? Don't go any further in this book until you master this concept.

Rejection is a myth. If you are denied a promotion, what have you lost? You are in the same spot you were before. You didn't have a promotion before you asked. Even though you didn't gain anything, no loss occurred either. Do not fear rejection. Learn to mentally catalog a "no" as a "not right now," instead of a "never." If an objective is important enough, you'll find a way.

When I was a controller at Smucker's, I needed another clerk in the accounting department. So I asked my manager if I could hire one. He said, "No." Instead of expressing sentiments of being overworked and upset at the decision, I went to work. I started with a complete analysis of the other facilities to compare staffing levels and activities. Then, we outlined areas where workload had increased over the years without adding additional staff. I sent the completed report to the Vice President, Richard Smucker. He said, "I knew you weren't going to go away." I didn't use his "no" as an excuse to fail. Instead, I brought him a workable solution. Subsequently, the additional staff was approved.

Your happiness and unhappiness are your responsibility. You have to own your good times as well as your bad times. If you don't like your circumstances, be accountable by creating a strategy to change them. No one is going to fix your life for you.

All too often we choose to claim the successes as our own and blame the failures on others or external circumstances. You tie up your energy. When you stop blaming, you can take that energy and redirect it. You can focus on shaping a better situation for yourself.

Leaders take responsibility for what they think, what they visualize and the actions they take. Don't waste your time and energy blaming and complaining. Evaluate your experiences and decide if a change is necessary. Face the uncomfortable and take risks to create the life you want to live.

Look at what you are complaining about and stop. "I'm overweight." "I have no time." "I owe too much money." "My friends and I are growing apart." "I'll never get married." "My spouse and I are just room-mates." Take inventory of your grievances. There's a good chance you can do something about them. Your complaints are about your dissatisfaction with your current situation, and you are feeling defeated. Blaming other people or giving up can't make the change you desire. It is up to you.

Take action! To transform your life, you must believe you can. Change your attitude and you'll get a different outcome. If you have already started on the path to change, make sure you have a plan for staying on track. It's up to you. Remember, excuses are the breakfast of victims; champions are fueled by action.

X

Make the Right Impression

The water I splashed on my face dripped off my chin as I stared at myself in the mirror. There will be no tears. Tears are a sign of weakness. You need to calm down. I took a deep breath, and at that moment, I took control. I refused to be a victim.

My boss and I had a heated discussion, and I felt defeated. I had excused myself to go to the restroom to try and pull myself together before I burst into tears. I was upset because I felt powerless. After taking a moment to collect myself, I returned to the meeting. I looked him in the eyes and said, "You're the boss. We'll do it your way."

By staying calm, I took away his power over me. In the end, he took my advice and backed away from his decision. As I matured, I learned to categorize these discussions mentally. They were business, not personal. It allowed me to control my emotions. It also left an impression on me when my boss changed his mind. By staying calm, I allowed him time to reconsider my perspective without making my view or emotions the focus.

Being able to remain calm under pressure isn't the only way to make the right impression. Consider your appearance. Times have changed. We live in a world where jeans are worn to church and work. It's easier to set yourself apart when you dress the part. The world says, "Don't judge a book by its cover." You and I both know that's a fantasy. We are judged every day, and while what others think doesn't define us, the way we present ourselves sends a message.

When making a sales pitch, I dress professionally and tastefully. I want my audience to focus on the message—not on my clothes. I want to exude confidence and professionalism. With my attire, I send a message that supports my mission of impressing upon them I'm the best person to do the job. That way, my words will support my appearance, and my appearance will also support my message.

I remember when a young man came to visit my office in a wrinkled T-shirt. He was making a sales call, and all I could think about was whether this was his personal best. I felt like it was, and it sent a message. If he didn't care about the way he looked how would he care for my business? He didn't think enough of the opportunity to look professional. There was no way I was going to do business with him.

Respect is earned, not given or awarded with a title. For example, there was a supervisor who would not replace her tennis shoes until they were worn out. After a few months, they became black and filthy. The supervisor led over 30 employees. She held team meetings to discuss the schedule, as well as cost, quality and service.

One day, an employee from her department visited my office to make an observation. He didn't have an HR problem. He said, "I have a hard time following her leadership and guidance on quality when her footwear says something else." He thanked me for listening and went back to work. The supervisor wasn't modeling her message resulting in a loss of respect.

When I met with her we discussed how a professional's appearance impacts the team's impression of her leadership. The changes she made allowed her to walk the walk in clean shoes.

I once had a director whose hair was always unkempt, long and without style. Although he was clean, he also regularly came to work in wrinkled clothes.

A director is paid around $150,000 annually. He could afford to look professional. We would host visitors, and he stood out. As the vice president, I was responsible for providing feedback to help my team achieve their personal best. He was a smart man. But the chief operating officer of the company never took him seriously because of his appearance. I scheduled a meeting to discuss the problem. I said, "Your hair and the way you dress is holding you back."

Since he was a brilliant person, he made the necessary changes immediately. He only needed scissors, a brush and an iron. No one ever pointed it out to him. He and his wife weren't good at ironing, so he used a dry cleaner with home delivery service to press his clothes for him. He kept his hair long but styled it. In the end, he thanked me for being frank with him.

Appearance really does matter. Find a style that works for you and tailor your appearance to fit you. For example, I wear colors that brighten my eyes. Vibrant colors make you appear less tired. I choose hues based upon whether my message is positive or negative. If the company performs well, I wear bright colors and my body language is welcoming. If corrections need to be made or something serious needs to be communicated, I wear dark colors. I make sure my body language is tight and on task.

As a leader, you must have the ability to communicate to a diverse audience. You'll have people you answer to on a regular basis and others who will answer to you. Treat them with respect and try to understand their perspective at all times.

Don't be quick to judge. Listen more than you talk. People just want to be heard. This concept is overlooked by many, but it is one of the best ways to make an impression in both your professional and personal life.

When people in power have the wrong perception of you, work on changing it. Discover what matters to them, and then try to be the solution they need. There is great value in the expression, "Never let them see you sweat." Leaders overcome obstacles, change perceptions, listen to the naysayers and then advance to prove them wrong. My success has always come from being a leader of people— not systems. I have strived to be a servant leader in order to develop relationships and build teams. If I'm here for them, they will be here for me. Dr. Martin Luther King Jr. said, "A genuine leader is not a searcher for consensus but a molder of consensus." What do you want to mold? If you control the message, you can control the impression, even in the eye of the storm.

X

Know Your Worth

For a large part of my life, I worked for corporate America. My mother ingrained a strong work ethic in her children. She taught us our most important boss is ourselves. Each day, I worked to make the company better. I went to bed every night knowing I put in a full day's work. I was in a constant state of learning and growing. Giving self-reviews or seeking constructive critique on a regular basis was important to keep myself in check. It's important for everyone to do these exercises. But it's more critical to do them right.

When you determine your worth, you have to balance the areas of greatness with the parts you can improve. We have all met people who are constantly self-deprecating. When they receive a compliment at work, they are quick to point out what they did wrong or how they could have performed better. They are public about what areas they need to improve.

On the other hand, there are those who think they can do no wrong. They don't accept advice or constructive coaching because they are so focused on how wonderful they are. You must find your balance between these two places.

The key to balance is to sing your praises, while you quietly work on personal growth. Tell others about your accomplishments and keep your shortcomings to yourself, while you work to get better in those areas. Be honest with yourself. While you are receiving criticism from others, be sure to give yourself compliments with "and" not "but." For example: "I need to work on increasing my sales, and I have already made 30 calls this week." This phrase sounds much better than, "I made 30 calls this week, BUT I still need to focus on increasing my sales." Instead of saying, "I lost 10 pounds, but I'm still fat." Change it to, "I lost 10 pounds, and I'm proud of my lifestyle changes."

The way you treat yourself is often the way others will treat you. If you only focus on how great you are, you'll become stagnant. Others will think you are a know-it-all, and you'll hinder opportunities to build good, solid relationships. If you only talk about what you could do better, or you give yourself average scores on self-reviews, those who have the power to promote you will follow your lead and see you as average.

Throughout my 30 years in corporate America, I continuously worked on my personal growth. I acknowledged my accomplishments, while working to improve. I was honest about where I was in my career and professional development.

I once had a director blame his poor performance on the company. His excuse was he had no prior experience before being promoted. I told him he alone was responsible for his lack of performance. By accepting the job, he committed to meeting expectations.

At the time, I was vice president for Coors Brewing Company. I explained if I was offered the CEO role, I was responsible for performing at that level if I accepted the job and benefits. He had been a manager but accepted the position and pay of director. But could not perform at that level. Many people have been promoted to a job they weren't qualified because they wanted the title and pay. The reality is the responsibility is shared. Companies do not have "on-the-job training" programs for directors or CEOs.

Many people are great at taking an honest inventory of their worth. But if you tend to struggle with giving yourself compliments, here is an exercise that will help. Describe the strengths of someone you admire in your career. You want to describe yourself the way they would describe themselves. Write it down. This becomes your personal elevator pitch.

Perhaps your chosen mentor is great with people. They are representing their company in a positive light and are always focused on helping the team. If those are the traits you admire, adopt them. It's a great litmus test for where you are in your career. Aim to be like the person you admire most. Build a résumé of accomplishments and quantifiable contributions.

You should maintain a running inventory in your head of all you have done to help your company. When I started in the business world, I knew I would need to establish relationships, and they needed to be genuine.

I worked for a man who didn't like me because of my gender and the color of my skin. He had never worked with a black female with a college education. He wasn't happy about it. To change his personal prejudices, I needed him to know my accomplishments in accounting. He wasn't interested in my wins, but I was determined to change his mind.

This level of personal prejudice and bias required me to be subtle. Otherwise, he would be openly annoyed and refuse to listen. So, I waited for him to discuss a topic to which I could relate. First, I stroked his ego. He needed that. Once I had him feeling good about himself, I would slip in information about a problem I solved. Of course, I gave him credit along the way. By the end of the first year, he told me I was the best accountant he had ever met.

As I grew, so did my contributing value. Mark Victor Hansen was co-creator of the New York Times best-selling book series, Chicken Soup for the Soul. He said, "When your self-worth goes up, your net worth goes up with it." That's what happened to me. As I grew, I was honest about my value and was willing to turn down an opportunity because it wasn't the right fit. But by the time I was offered a new position with Coors, I knew my value exceeded the salary I was offered. I made great money, but I was worth more than they would pay me. So, I later started my own company, worked hard and I now earn what I'm worth.

To know your true value, you must understand your competition. Sometimes, it's a co-worker. Other times, it's the little voice in your head whispering, You're not good enough. Take inventory of where you are and be honest. Don't toot your horn louder than it deserves to blow, but don't keep silent if you've done something great. Focus on growth, while you give yourself lots of compliments. When you master knowing your worth, you won't have to wait on anybody else to push or pull you into your future. You'll lead yourself.

Stand Out

Great things happen when you set yourself up to be noticed in the right ways. What if you could stand out in a crowded field and be seen as the successful entrepreneur, servant leader, budding professional or exceptional talent that you are?

It is possible for others to accept you at your personal best. It is also critical to stand out as you climb the corporate ladder or deliver exceptional results.

As I shared before, I started with the J. M. Smucker Company as a staff accountant. My first day at work, I met the accounting team. No one looked like me. They were all women, but they were also all white. Nita, the office manager, introduced me as the new accounting clerk—not the accountant.

At first, I thought it was a mistake. I soon realized she didn't want to acknowledge my title. She certainly didn't want to recognize my accomplishment as a degreed accountant. As time went on, I began to understand that acknowledging my title and education made her feel small. She couldn't admit I was a smart, educated, 20-year-old black woman. She had a mental picture of a black woman. Regardless of my accomplishments, it's how she saw me.

When I share this story with young professionals or entrepreneurs, I emphasize it was HER problem, not mine. Her values didn't become my values. Instead, I saw it as a challenge. Like my mother before me, I had a torch to carry. It was up to me to knock down the barrier that Nita and others had created. In order to affect change, I needed to build relationships that would change the attitude of my all-Caucasian team. I had to educate them on the reality of my ability and refocus their attention from the color of my skin. If I succeeded, they would become comfortable working with members of the black community.

My mother taught me to set my own values, and I did. At first, I stood out, but for all the wrong reasons.

It definitely wasn't for my intelligence and contributions. But I was determined.

I arrived at work every day knowing Nita viewed me as a threat. She openly ridiculed me with others who appeared like-minded. Regardless, my daily interactions with everyone were positive. I didn't allow their poor character to affect mine. I showed up at least 30 minutes early each morning. I planned my day with a level of professionalism and confidence.

During my first year, I was a sponge. I learned all the business processes at Smucker's. For example, I learned our computer programming language. It allowed me to help troubleshoot problems. I became an asset to the Orrville, Ohio, accounting team because I was hungry to learn more. I became a standout as a continuous learner with the willingness to support others.

My passion for life continued to attract the team to me. My positive attitude was contagious, which drew people to me. My supportive attitude, willingness to listen and integrity were crucial for building relationships. These characteristics even helped me connect with people who were determined not to like me. I learned if you can provide value to others, they will seek you out for help. It is critical for you to make team members comfortable with you. Don't make them feel dumb. Your goal is for others to view you as approachable, so they seek your guidance in the future. I wanted to be a standout by being inspirational, while using my life examples as my message.

Several people would not speak with me regardless of my friendly approach. I was consistent in my behavior by smiling and greeting everyone daily. These employees would look at me and keep walking, but I didn't allow them to impact my positive attitude and work ethic. Every day, I radiated positive energy to everyone. I took the time to assist associates with any problems, whether at my local plant or at other facilities.

I became the go-to person for information about the facility and accounting issues. I made myself essential. So regardless of prejudice, people would have to acknowledge my value to the company. For example, I learned simple thing, like the customer's filing system.

I'm naturally curious. In a non-threating and respectful manner, I asked the records clerk to walk me through the system. She felt honored when I showed genuine interest in her work. I demonstrated respect and appreciation for her knowledge. She was happy to teach me what I wanted to know.

Most days, I stayed until 6 p.m. If someone in sales called and needed to know about a customer order, I was there to help. They were surprised I knew how to access the information. Since I learned to retrieve what they needed from the records clerk, I had all the data to answer their questions.

There was still work to be done. I needed to build relationships with the all-white management team. They didn't see the value of adding me to the Memphis team. They felt that I was a token black female to meet their Equal Employment Opportunity Commission "EEOC" requirements, which counted as two points. I decided I would prove my value to them. There were seven managers from whom I wanted to gain respect. I started to attend open meetings. I listened to their conversations about problems at the facility. Keep in mind, they talked freely about everything. They saw me as a nobody. During these discussions, I was most interested in issues they couldn't solve.

I selected several long-term problems that would get me noticed. I didn't want anyone to know I was working to solve these problems. It was my habit to take lunch at my desk. I tried to stay under the radar, so I always used my lunch hour, when everyone was gone so I could work on the issues.

For months, I collected data to determine if there were any trends in quality control issues. Was the first batch of jelly soft every Monday? When we cleaned the machines, did we lose money getting back up and running? Every problem became an opportunity for me.

As I developed solutions, employees and managers became comfortable working with me. I always gave credit for success to the team. I treated managers and hourly employees the same by giving them equal recognition. My actions prevented anyone from feeling threatened, while motivating everyone to continue working with me.

Remember standing out requires you to set yourself up to be noticed in the right ways. Everyone needs a friend at work, a resource for questions or a good listener. It requires you to use your leadership skills to lead both laterally and bilaterally. In the end, I showed them I was more than two points on an EEOC report. I worked extra hard to be noticed in a positive way. And it was my thirst for knowledge and the relationships that I developed that made me the entrepreneur I am today.

Great things happen when you set yourself up to stand out in a crowd. Regardless of any bias, it is possible to change perceptions if you remain positive, do the work, put in the effort and add value. In the end, you won't just stand out. You'll be outstanding.

X

Don't Let Bad News Age

Delicate information is not like fine wine. It doesn't improve with age. Great leaders are able to handle tough situations and have the character to deliver bad news. The problem could be a mistake that causes pain or damage, end a bad relationship or terminate someone's employment. If you want to be a leader, you can't stick your head in the sand. It is best to address tough situations head on and with integrity. How you handle the hard stuff leaves an impression on people.

Whenever I waited to tell my mother bad news about my siblings' actions, she said I was as guilty as the person who committed the act. I also violated her trust by keeping the secret. If a problem is discovered before you communicate it to the right person, they won't trust you to be honest in the future. Lack of credibility could result in a customer or superior constantly looking over your shoulder. The lack of trust is even worse in your personal life.

I once had a major supplier who billed us for product we didn't receive. His packages didn't arrive full, yet we were charged for full cases. He was insulted when we contacted him about this discrepancy. To make matters worse, the suppliers' Chief Operating Officer was the golfing buddy of my Chief Operating Officer. I had to tread lightly when I brought this issue to his attention. Challenging an executive's friend the wrong way could have been a career-ending move. Instead, we ended the supplier's contract. The relationship between the two men ended, as well.

My boss knew he could not continue to associate with members of this organization. He thanked me for my professionalism, vigilance, follow-up and thoroughness. I impressed him when I tactfully made the tough step of letting him know his friend lacked integrity. After that incident, he promoted me three times. He took notice of my professionalism, integrity, attention to detail and thoroughness. He knew I had the character and intelligence to become the company's first black female plant manager.

Could he have taken action against me? Sure. But I wouldn't be able to sleep at night if I had let the problem continue. Dr. Martin Luther King Jr. once said, "Our lives begin to end the day we become silent about things that matter." The company who was underfilling our shipments would have had control over me with this secret. As my mom said many times, my silence would have allowed their values to impact my values. You must hold tight to your integrity. It's imperative if you want to lead well.

Leaders also know that the first person to report the problem provides an opportunity to control the time, place and quality of the communications. When discussing an issue, talk to the person on the phone or in person. It's nearly impossible to have a meaningful conversation through email, text message or Facebook. The telephone call conveys the message is important and gives them time to speak or vent. It gives you the platform to provide positive reassurance. This timely, open conversation minimizes misunderstanding by providing clear, concise details. Come clean as soon as possible to prevent a perception of deceit or cover-up. Transparency is the best way to form a solid foundation for relationships. When you come clean, be prepared with a solution if possible.

When I found myself in this situation, I always gave a detailed description of the planned corrective action. I also advised the customer that we would make them whole if there was money involved.

On one occasion, we had a valve fail, which caused $40,000 worth of energy drink to go down the sewer drain, literally. I developed a solution and notified the customer right away. I explained the system failure and assured them we would pay for the loss. I told them we checked inventory and verified suppliers could immediately ship the remaining ingredients at our expense. I closed by telling them the order would only be a day late. Mistakes happen. But we never lost a client for coming clean. Instead, many customers told us we were one of the few companies they trusted.

We understood honesty, timely communications and providing a workable solution were a direct reflection of our integrity.

Years ago, my daughter Whitney ran her car through our garage into the dining room. She knew I was rehearsing for a major speech, which would be attended by the Secretary of Labor for the United States. She called me anyway. She told me she wasn't hurt, and the damage was minor. After my son arrived home from school, he called me. "Mom, it's not a little damage," he said. "The wall is busted open, and the new china cabinet has a hole in the back. It was pushed a few feet into the room."

Whitney's communication style is truthful, but she'll minimize details. Christopher's style is to state the facts clearly and in a timely manner. Unlike my siblings during my childhood, Christopher didn't hold his sister hostage. They both understood my parenting style and knew it was important to call me immediately. They trusted I would not overreact.

Different people have different communication styles. Two employees may observe the same incident. One employee's description leads you to believe the world is on fire. Another provides the same facts but gives minimum details with an unemotional tone, which says it's minor. What differs is their personalities and their experiences, which influences their perspectives. Knowing the style of your child, employee or coworker helps you interpret the real message.

The longer you wait to share bad news, the more stress you'll experience. As you try to hide something or fix it before people find out, it will take its toll on you. Emotions are like a volcano. The more the pressure builds up, the larger the eruption. It's better to handle a crisis right away by discussing it with the right people. Then, you can focus all of your energy on overcoming whatever problem you are facing.

Simon Sinek, an author and great leader said, "More information is always better than less. When people know the reason things happen, even if it's bad news, they can adjust their expectations and react accordingly. Keeping people in the dark only serves to stir negative emotions." When leaders "Look Up" and own their mistakes, others will learn to "Look Up," as well. Control the message, and you have taken your first step toward handling the problem.

Great leaders can lead in the sunlight, as well as in the rain. Most often, it's in the storm where they hone their leadership skills. In the end, waiting too long leaves the relationship spoiled. No matter what, be sure to "Look Up." There is a solution on the horizon once you get past the delivery of the bad news.

Build Relationships

Being an entrepreneur is not a breeding ground for equality. Women and minorities start the race with less capital. People are less likely to take a chance on us. It contributes to higher failure rates for new businesses. It was my experience when I started my first company.

I don't suffer the affliction of not needing help. We all need a hand. It takes a village to succeed. I receive support from the relationships I've developed, which I call "human collateral." It occurs when individuals invest in others. They do it by providing advice or help. I use relationships established on more than 20 boards over the past 20 years. My human collateral account has a nice portfolio of connections.

White males create human collateral through friendships. They do it at college, in fraternities, at work or through other organizations. These relationships develop while golfing, having drinks or attending after-work social events. They use these associations to gain confidential information. They call on their friends to steer decisions to benefit the business relationship. A man can leverage relationships he built through these types of interactions the rest of his life. The police call it the brotherhood, while fraternities have a secret code. Men, in general, use this game. They will take their human collateral to a new job or assignment. They keep it close for life.

While I was at Smucker's, there was a service company that was critical to our success. Stan was the representative, and he made his own schedule. It meant he could choose which companies received the most support. I learned that Stan loved barbecue and sports. He especially loved Michael Jordan. Whenever Stan was in town, I took him to Corky's BBQ. The entire lunch, he talked about Michael Jordan and his team. As a result, I started watching the Chicago Bulls. I learned a lot about Michael Jordan and was able to speak intelligently about the games. I invested my time in Stan's passions. It created human collateral that brought Stan to Memphis six times in one year. At no cost to our company, he provided additional training, which enabled my team to perform better. Stan shared information and tips he rarely disclosed to others. I was able to maintain a valuable relationship for future support with some friendly conversation and the cost of a simple dinner.

Later in my career at Coors, a co-worker was promoted to senior vice president and had to fire his best friend. They had worked together at other companies. He recommended his hiring. He was his golfing buddy and the godfather of his children. The co-worker knew this manager had significant performance issues. But this relationship was an unbreakable bond. He obviously owed a lot of human collateral. He assisted his friend in securing a higher-paying job. He also gave him a year's salary to leave. He did his job and saved the relationship. He created human collateral.

During my career, I made it my mission to build human collateral with CEOs and COOs. I did the same with their administrative assistants. I always stopped at their desk with small talk about their children. I knew the kids' names, if they were in college, sports and/or key points from our last conversations. I would ask for their opinions on topics to show my respect for them and their position. I did it to gain access to the executive level for brief conversations or meetings. I could call them to see if the executive was in a good mood. This helped me determine an optimal time to ask for capital dollars or share bad news. These relationships helped my success because timing is everything.

Many times, people don't acknowledge the janitor or receptionist. These employees get treated as if they are invisible. Albert Einstein once said, "I speak to everyone in the same way, whether he is the garbage man or the president of the University." I do the same. My mother taught we are all equal, no matter our position. And these "invisible" people provided my best intelligence information. They moved around and heard important conversations. Executives didn't bother to limit what they said in front of them. They didn't consider these people important. Remember, we may not see them, but they see and hear everything.

Human collateral built prior to starting my first company became critical. It ensured my business, Hardy

Bottling, came before major corporations. I often received free service from equipment technicians during other service visits in my area. These relationships often gave me months to pay for parts. Additionally, they used their beverage relationships to promote my business needs: human collateral. It gave me access to services that were necessary for my survival.

Women and minorities must understand the human collateral game and use it to build a portfolio of relationships. Historically, many women have not enjoyed the same camaraderie. They have not been as quick to create networks of other women.

I tell my team that I do a lot of favors for people and rarely accept a check. When you pay me, it will be for something I can't provide for myself. I treat my human collateral as a precious asset. I'm slow to call in a favor. I wait until I need something big.

Human collateral requires your time in order to build relationships. You must be strategic in your use of authority. Show respect for those outside your inner circle. The relationships you build today will hurt you or help you in the future. It's hard to lead, but it's even harder to lead alone.

Understand Personalities

Mark Twain said, "The difference between the right word and the almost right word is the difference between lightning and a lightning bug." How you communicate is important, but you must also understand the different personalities on your team.

Years ago, I had a supervisor who was hated by his team and many other employees. His demeanor wasn't friendly, and his natural looks screamed, "Don't bother me." When he spoke to his team to ask questions or give directions, he appeared to bark at them. Whenever his manager was absent, this department reported to me. One day, I witnessed the supervisor, Gary, having a meltdown. There was a problem that stopped the entire operation. I was with the plant manager, Dick, and we observed the interaction while we stood overhead.

Gary saw a problem and raced to the employee. He appeared to be in a rage as he yelled at the worker. The conversation was super animated. The employee nodded his head in acknowledgment of the oversight. The packaging supervisor was repeatedly paging Gary to tell him he needed product. The commotion made matters worse. We continued to stand overhead and watched the entire facility at a standstill, which created stress for Gary. He yelled at other employees to move faster to get the operation running. Employees ran left and right to get the "wheels" back on.

The plant manager asked me to fire Gary immediately. He felt his interpersonal skills were inexcusable. I told Dick that once Gary's manager returned from vacation, he could terminate Gary. In the interim, I met with Gary to let him explain what caused the operation to come to a halt.

When he finished describing the problem, I discussed our concerns with his interpersonal skills. I told him about the lack of professionalism demonstrated on the shop floor. He said Dick made him nervous. He thought his aggressive behavior is what the plant manager expected. I explained that his role as a leader was to remain calm—not fall apart—in the face of a storm. He returned to work, but I emphasized that such behavior was unacceptable and could result in termination.

His relationship with the team needed to improve, but it was critical for Gary to lead the change. I faced a challenge. The plant manager wanted to react like Gary. His response was emotional. I knew to be successful, cooler heads must prevail. It's how my mother handled every adversity that came her way.

After the meeting with Gary, I immediately met with Dick. I shared Gary's explanation for his actions. I explained he modeled his leadership style after the plant manager. Dick became upset stating the explanation wasn't true. I told him I hated to be the bearer of bad news, but Gary was correct. I observed his overbearing manner many times.

After I shared this information, I returned to my office. He needed time to reflect upon his failure to lead by example. Gary kept his job, and the plant manager became less overbearing.

Later that year, the company sponsored a softball team. They were winning, and the employee morale was at an all-time high. I promised to attend the last two games of the season. The interesting thing about this team was Gary was their coach. As a supervisor, he had a bad disposition and was unapproachable. But as a coach, he inspired the team, and the players respected him. Where was supervisor Gary and who was this coach that looked like him?

As a coach, Gary consulted the team. He accepted their input. He inspired confidence in the group, which helped each member perform at their personal best. He voiced positive appreciation for effort and initiative. I finally understood what had changed. The team had an opportunity to meet and appreciate the real Gary. He was approachable, inclusive and a team player. He was the same Gary, but the team accepted his loud voice, stoic face and nervous twitch. They saw his heart, which minimized his personal imperfections. They accepted Gary for himself. Gary recognized his teammates' hearts, passion, energy and personalities. This newfound respect for each other expanded to the workplace, and the relationship between Gary and his team improved.

My mother raised 14 children with a wide assort-
ment of personalities. There were introverts and extro-
verts. My siblings and I were a mix of docile, intense,
aggressive, dependable, courageous and suspicious. She
had at least one of each. She valued and loved each
unique personality. The guidance she provided was
based on each child's individual needs. My mother knew
how to communicate with each of us to inspire us to
give our best. I'm still in awe of her leadership abilities
when I think of how critical this skill was to the success
of my family.

I have three children, each with a different personality. They are all highly educated professionals. My
oldest, Jennifer, has been mature since she was five
years old. She holds herself accountable. She is a per-
fectionist who never breaks the rules. She was a kind,
loving child, but not aggressive enough. Other kids
would push her around. She was placed in situations that
forced her to take a position or find common ground.
She learned to adapt, without losing her kindness in
those situations. She took charge as a teenager by managing the house and watching her siblings in my absence. As an adult she uses those same skills in her

career. She is comfortable challenging tough situations and she is a great leader.

My middle child, Whitney, is brilliant and creative. She finds boundaries and then works to move them. Knowing her personality, I gave her strict rules as a child. My instructions to her were always clear because she would interpret whatever she wanted from our communications. But her creative interpretation is what fueled a desire to think outside of the box. The defense of her position allowed her to become a great communicator. I never wanted to stifle her out-of-the-box thinking and communication skills as she grew up. Today, the boundaries she moves have enabled her to succeed in her career.

My son Christopher is analytical, structured and a brilliant strategist. He strives for perfection and also holds himself accountable. If he wants something, he will put in the work. He is not going to break the rules but will challenge a person in authority if he thinks they are wrong. Since he was going to test his teacher regardless of what I said, I taught him that it's not what you say but how you say it." He learned to be professional but direct.

My parenting goal wasn't to change my children's personalities but to provide them the guidance they needed to mature with optimal outcomes. My husband and I wanted to foster the best parts of their unique personalities and gently tame the elements that could hold them back.

I recommend professionals and entrepreneurs attend networking events. Get to know your potential clients or employees in a relaxed environment, as the softball team did. We are all just people under our titles. Each of us has feelings, dreams and aspirations. Get to know the people around you. Learn what makes them tick and, in the end, it will be easier to develop real, meaningful relationships. This lesson will be important as you further your professional goals. It doesn't matter if you are just starting out in your career or already running your own company. It is never too late to invest in this skill.

Great leaders are always looking for an opportunity to interact with their team. It allows them to understand and appreciate individual personalities. An investment in an employee is an investment in the company. An investment in a coworker or target is an investment in your career. And as you learn about one another, it will make your life and their lives better—regardless of the professional impact.

Don't Leave Dead Bodies

In my experience, there are two types of yelling. One puts fear in you, and one encourages the development of the spirit. My mom was a pro at the latter. She rarely yelled at us. And when she did, she always explained mistakes and administered the appropriate punishment. If the infraction wasn't severe, we would lose a privilege, such as going outside. She felt it was punishment enough for us to hear the others playing, while we remained inside.

My mother communicated in a way that engaged us. Even when we were getting into trouble, she explained the lesson to be learned. She rarely raised her voice. She knew if she spent all her time merely pointing out our mistakes, it would kill our spirits or, as I like to say, she would be "leaving dead bodies." That's what happens when you spew criticism without regard for how it might hinder the situation or person.

During my years at Coors, I encountered a lot of "dead bodies." The workforce was angry and often disrespected each other. There were many grievances written for employees cursing at management or other employees. It was a caustic work environment with excessive absenteeism. With this barrage of negative energy, words and attitudes, I could only imagine employees dreaded coming to work each day.

That was the carnage I faced when I became vice president at Coors. If progress was to be made, the communication barriers needed to be dealt with immediately. It was the first step to improve the facility's performance. A company is only as great as its people, and a team can't shine when they feel violated.

Coors was unionized, so I followed contract protocols. I met with union representatives to communicate the policy change to address the negative behavior running rampant throughout the company. I was cognizant that my message needed to be delivered by me in back-to-back meetings. My objective was to deliver a forceful and decisive directive. The scheduling eliminated the risk of a second-hand, watered-down version of what I needed them to hear.

I decided to call a town hall meeting. These are commonly used by companies to communicate relevant information to all levels of the organization and to gain feedback from participants. The meeting was about mutual respect. My role as vice president was to create a safe and positive work environment to achieve desired company results.

At the meeting, I discussed my concern with the abusive, disrespectful and bullying behavior. Employee morale and productivity were at an all-time low. I observed people doing everything possible to avoid speaking with others. A 30-second problem would go on for minutes, creating thousands of units of rejected product versus a few hundred. The hope was the other person would notice the issue rather than having to point it out to them.

I apologized to the 90 percent of the workforce who were either abused or forced to work in a caustic environment. Even though most of the employees didn't contribute to the problems, many suffered from the consequences. I explained management had failed them and the behavior would stop immediately. The past penalty for this infraction was either no punishment or a three-day suspension. The offenders accepted the consequences as a slap on the wrist. It was ineffective.

I told the team "In a safety zone where roadwork is in process, the fines for speeding are extreme. The penalty is designed to get your attention to discourage speeding. It works." I said, "In the future, these behaviors will result in immediate termination." There was dead silence. I added, "This punishment applies to everyone who works for me," which was everyone in the facility, including management.

The next day, I hosted my monthly luncheon meeting with supervisors and managers. A supervisor said I would not follow through with my threat. I said, "If I have to fire a single person to maintain my credibility with 650 employees, I will fire that individual in a heartbeat. A leader's integrity and credibility are priceless, since your word must be your bond. If I were you, I would not be the first to test this new penalty."

In less than a month, management observed two salaried employees in a cursing match. They had been warned. Without hesitation, I terminated them. They filed a complaint with corporate for wrongful termination. The firings were upheld.

Within the same month, an hourly employee verbally assaulted someone in housekeeping with racial slurs. He wanted to use the restroom closed for cleaning. Instead of being polite and respectful, he resorted to intimidation. The results were housekeeping did the minimum amount of work as fast as possible to avoid further encounters. Since the housekeeping team was outsourced, not addressing this behavior was a negative reflection on the company. The employee was immediately terminated. His firing went through the entire grievance process, which included arbitration.

My speech was presented as evidence that the policy change process adhered to the contract. Hourly employees were concerned the employee would win. I encouraged them to notify the union, which they funded, of their concern. They were more comfortable speaking with the vice president.

During the meeting, I said to the employees "Your interaction with others is leaving dead bodies. It is not only creating an unfriendly work environment, but it prohibits people from accomplishing their goals. The negative get-in-your-face approach or negative body language causes individuals to find every excuse to avoid communication. This is leaving dead bodies because it is human nature to seek any excuse to never speak to the negative."

How many dead bodies have you left in your wake? How many opportunities have you missed because of them? Is there a way to make sure you never do it again?

Michelle Obama said it best, "When they go low, we go high." I believe if we embrace the First Lady's approach as we walk through life, our own experiences will be better. I will continue to encourage communication that develops the spirit, which makes for better results all around. When others go low, I will continue to go high. I invite you to do the same.

X

Never Let a Good Problem Go to Waste

After my freshman year in college, I enrolled in an English class in summer school to complete my basic class requirements. I paid the tuition with savings from my part-time job. The first day of class, the professor announced that black students should leave because they will be disappointed with their grade. I had never heard anyone say out loud that I was going to fail because I was black. Every black student left, except me. I paid for the course with my hard-earned money, so I was going to attend class each day.

The first day of class, I sat near the back. After his announcement, I arrived early to sit in the front row. The least I could get was the satisfaction of making him uncomfortable. By sitting in the front, he was forced to look at me for several hours each day. When he asked a question, I always raised my hand. He would ignore me, so I waved it back and forth. He used his grading authority to isolate black students. I exercised my right to make his life miserable for the summer. My goal was to teach him the consequences of making his statement. In the future, he may encounter another Carolyn. At the end of the summer, he gave me a C for my English grade. I earned an A+ in taking back my power.

There are many different ways I could have handled the situation. I could have quit the course and told myself the situation was hopeless. I could have taken it personally. Instead, I took control of the problem. I stayed in the class and made sure the professor felt my presence. In the end, I faced the adversity and came out stronger and smarter on the other side.

Sitting in that class with an overtly racist teacher was practice for what I would face later in life. When I'm handed lemons, I sit back and enjoy a chilled glass of lemonade. It's the smartest way to approach a problem. Issues are practice sessions for leaders. We learn by trial and error, which demonstrates we can think on our feet. If there were no problems, leaders wouldn't be needed. I have a favorite saying after a hard time, "Leaders are hired and paid for the tough days. The easy ones are gifts and serve as a little bonus."

After four years on the job, Coors announced my plant was closing. It was no surprise when our quality and efficiency severely declined. Employees weren't focused, and the wheels fell off our well-oiled machine. People were upset. They no longer felt they had a vested interest in the job. It was hard to blame them. In less than 30 days we experienced the worst quality losses in the plant's history.

Even though we were in a tough situation, I still had a job to do. I needed to find creative ways to refocus employees and direct their minds off the closing. I called a town hall meeting to make an announcement to our team members.

I explained we were going to compete for the company's Environmental Health and Safety award. I told the team if they won, I would present the trophy to Leo Kiely III, CEO of Coors Brewing Company. It would be a symbol of our greatness and show him the mistake he made in closing the Memphis facility. "Team, we have an opportunity to go out on top. Let's not allow this closing to be your legacy. Let's set our own. We will compete for this award and we will win." The employees looked at me like I had fallen on my head.

The Memphis plant's performance was consistently last since the creation of the award. They had never tried to win because they considered it an impossible task. We would be graded in 18 different categories.

We knew the Shenandoah, VA plant always won, but the team had become complacent. They never saw it coming when we buckled down and went to work to replace them at the top.

Our strategy was to assign each category to a manager to focus their full attention on winning. We were going to divide and conquer. We worked aggressively to earn all available training points. Our strategy was to present them to corporate the last week of the contest. We waited until the end to prevent drawing attention to ourselves. We won! It was a source of embarrassment for Coors but a point of pride for all my employees.

It took the company a month to announce the victory, since it was unexpected. They could not find a reason to disqualify our win. In addition, my employees earned a significant quarterly bonus, since many of the areas impacted financial metrics. I could not let a good problem go to waste. A plant closing is considered the end of an era—like a death. Most people would coast until the doors shut. It's not how you lead. Instead, I used it to inspire the team to do the impossible at the lowest point in their lives. Our performance improved because we chose success. We turned a huge problem into our greatest advantage.

Another example is employee benefits. They are a great example of complexity, especially health care options. Hourly employees didn't understand them. They didn't trust they would select the best benefit plan. Many would choose not to sign up for insurance coverage because the process intimidated them. When they ignored signing up for insurance, it impacted them because they were less likely to go to the doctor or they would stress because they had no coverage when they needed it. I had to communicate the benefit information in a way they would understand. The problem represented an opportunity to build trust. I was able to explain everything in a way that wasn't intimidating or degrading. They got their health coverage and the company had happy employees.

We all face problems. Focus on the impact the solution will have when the issue is resolved. Then plan a way to get there. A great leader is able to turn a crisis into an opportunity. Leaders know that ultimately the problem is not the problem. They must learn to focus on the solution instead. Learn this lesson and put your out-of-the-box thinking to work. Make it happen. Remember, as you look for opportunities to shine, never let a good problem go to waste.

X

Be the Change You Wish to See

Many people go antique shopping as a hobby—looking through old dusty warehouses of treasures from another time. As long as my mother lived, she never had a desire to shop for antiques. All of her belongings were old and had always belonged to someone else first. Some of our furniture was even picked up off the side of the road. My mother's dream was to buy something new.

After her youngest child started kindergarten, she took control. She successfully applied for a job as a school custodian. She saved her earnings and bought a brand-new sofa and loveseat. She was so proud of her furniture, she covered it in plastic. It still sits preserved in the living room of her old home. She never wanted to replace it. She took pride in working hard to earn something. She lived by the philosophy, "If you want great things to come into your life, you better go out there and start working for them." As a result, she became the change she wished to see in our family.

This desire for continuous improvement and learning has been the cornerstone of my career. At every job, in every position, I saw areas where the company could improve. I wanted each organization to be the best it could be regardless of my title. This critical mindset contributed significantly to my success. By looking for ways to improve, I was able to stand out to my superiors. I was able to help co-workers when they needed it, and I learned more in the process. I determined who I wanted to be at each company and then I developed a strategy to get there.

I observed the leadership qualities of people in positions of authority. I made mental notes on the pros and cons of their leadership skills. I worked to sharpen my skills in those areas. I listened to people from other departments to learn what made their jobs difficult and asked them for ideas to improve their job. My role was to lead them to think outside the box. I made sure to give

150 percent to the job I was hired to do. I put in extra time by working longer hours and learning as much as I could during my lunch breaks. I became the change I wanted to see at my company.

I wasn't asked to lead, but I did. I wasn't looking for fanfare. I was hoping to become better. I knew this would lead to change. Making positive changes by working hard would propel my career.

Early on, I made a lateral job move to quality manager. After holding the position for less than a year, we performed a loss analysis. The company was losing a significant amount of money due to operational issues. It had been acceptable for years. I was determined to change this attitude of mediocrity. During our annual meeting with the CEO, I boldly set a goal to cut our losses in half within one year. My team almost fainted after the announcement.

Based on my analysis of historical data, I learned our problems followed the 80/20 rule. The data revealed that over 80 percent of our quality problems were isolated to a single category. Therefore, we tackled that category first. We involved employees through inclusion and training. An analysis of each issue was completed to determine the root cause. All discovery was shared with the team. It created excitement since everyone liked to win. Employee's knowledge of corrective actions prevented these issues from reoccurring. I focused our efforts on developing processes to do it right the first time. And we did. Then, I moved on to the next issue. I crossed each problem off the list for a year.

After 12 months of hard work, the team accomplished this lofty goal. We transformed the plant's history of low expectations and performance. The team became the change agent by creating a new legacy of performing at higher standards.

Great leaders also create a compelling vision. When it happens, a team will follow that leader with passion and blind conviction. As I worked my way up the ladder, people started to understand my vision was for our company to be the best. My excitement was contagious. When others noticed my success making changes, they wanted to become a part of the journey. People in different departments started coming to me for solutions.

Sharing my vision helped build relationships along the way. It also led me to a promotion to plant manager. It wasn't necessarily a good thing. I wasn't sure how long I would maintain the job because I quickly realized the facility was in trouble. Our plant was spending more money to produce than any other location in the company. Production would be transferred or our facility would be shut down. We needed to fix the problem.

We developed strategies to improve efficiencies and reduce waste to cut costs. We were the first facility to run on a 24-hour schedule. To improve flexibility, we cross-trained employees to do other jobs. Our efficiency increased, and we reduced our cost below other company facilities.

We made these changes under the radar. While no one was watching, the plant that spent the most became the plant that spent the least. The corporate executive team was shocked.

Even after we made the improvements, there was a rumor that our plant was still going to close. I inquired about the rumor and was told the company was "reducing capacity." That was a roundabout way of confirming the rumors were true.

The plant closing consultants needed accounting and operations expertise. I filled this role, since I was a CPA as well as a plant manager. Within two weeks, I constructed capacity and cost models to evaluate all facilities. During the CEO's review of our analysis, he asked why the corporate facility was excluded. He wanted all facilities evaluated. There were no sacred cows. The project initially depressed me, since I felt my plant was the target. After the scope was expanded to include all plants, I felt the playing field was level.

The consultant's recommendation was to reduce capacity at the corporate facility. My location was spared because it had become the low-cost producer. My drive for continuous improvements and the team's willingness to change saved over 150 jobs.

As a leader, you have to keep your eye on the prize. Great leaders see the big picture, as well as the crucial details. If you want to be an agent for change, stay focused and avoid corporate drama or petty politics. When you know where you want to go, make sure your feet are taking you in that direction. I have worked with leaders who chased ants, while the business was run over by elephants. Most of my accomplishments started as elephants—requiring me to eat problems one bit at a time.

Mom trained us to believe the only failure in life is not trying. I'm amazed by how many people talk themselves out of greatness. They have a brilliant idea, but they quickly convince themselves, "It will never work." Amazingly, people give fear of failure more power than the rewards of success.

Great leaders have a vision, which they go after. They MAKE it happen. If you want to grow and go after something, do it. Don't make getting noticed your primary focus; focus on being the best in everything you do or finding solutions that evade others. As Harriett Tubman once said, "Every great dream begins with a dreamer. Always remember, you have within you the strength, the patience and the passion to reach for the stars to change the world." Great leaders are "wired" to make a difference. It is part of their DNA.

$\mathbb{X}$

Use Your Education, Lean on Common Sense

If you ever get a chance to sit in a major airport and quietly watch, you'll quickly realize people have short fuses. I've witnessed some pretty atrocious behavior. I've come to the realization that common sense is not so common.

When a flight is canceled, it's frustrating. I observed people harassing the ticket agent. Anyone with common sense knows a ticket agent has no control over the flight cancellation. The moment the announcement was made, I realized alternate flights would be limited.

I quickly got on my phone and booked another seat before the other angry customers stopped yelling at the agent. I used common sense to solve the problem. The decision to wave your arms and yell will leave your feet on the ground, while you wait for the next open seat. It's a waste of time.

Car repair shops, used car sales reps and contractors have a reputation for preying on people who lack common sense or experience. The friendly, caring manner can sometimes be an act. They may be trying to convince you the best deal is in front of you. Many customers mentally buy into a skilled salesman approach to gain their trust. Common sense should tell you that their priority is the company's bottom line. Your satisfaction may be second to their profits.

The definition of common sense is sound and prudent judgment based on a simple perception of the situation or facts. As a leader, you have to consider the situation and facts when making decisions.

You can't rely solely on your education, personal feelings or a set of rules. Remember, you are dealing with humans. Your common sense will be important when you decide what policies to break or which ones to follow in a given situation.

There are so many brilliant people who teach our children. Great educators use both common sense and education skills to work miracles in the lives of young people. Unfortunately, there are also educators who lack sound judgment. They sometimes make comments to students and parents that are inappropriate. They may not realize the emotional impact their words have on those on the receiving end.

My sister's high school teacher stereotyped Debra because of our large family. She told her she wouldn't have a successful career and expected her to live in the housing projects with "lots of babies." This teacher was leaning on stereotypes. An educator's role is to teach, motivate and uplift young minds. Her lack of common sense, coupled with personal prejudices, caused her to verbalize her personal feelings.

Those words challenged my sister. Debra encountered this teacher years later. She reminded her former teacher of the prediction she made. Debra told her she became a teacher and had received many accolades for education and coaching. The teacher walked away without responding.

When common sense is coupled with an excellent education, you have the recipe for handling some of the toughest situations as a leader. Successful leaders learn to balance education and common sense. Like the scales of justice, the balance between education and common sense swings based upon each unique situation.

If you earn a college education or learn a trade, you own these credentials. No one can take them away. When a company downsizes, those impacted the most are people without education and marketable skills. For example, if a hospital downsizes, nurses and doctors will immediately find other positions. But those working in housekeeping may find it tougher to secure a job with equal pay.

Throughout my career, I worked in union environments. The United Steelworkers define a union as a group of people working together to improve their work lives through collective bargaining. As a vice president, I learned the Teamsters' chief union steward thought he was smarter than everyone, including company leaders. He had been in control of the company and union in my location for over 10 years. It was about to change.

My education and ability to review detailed contracts allowed me to analyze problems. I used common sense and relationships to learn who he had failed to represent. I soon found them on my side. The managers were more afraid of him than of upper management. I learned from my first mentor, sometimes fear is necessary. In this case, I used it to get the managers back on my side. Regaining control of the leadership team was critical. As a result, those who didn't believe the operation could change were terminated during the organization's restructuring. The remaining managers understood that change was mandatory.

Common sense and education came in handy when a tornado caused over $50 million in damage to my bottling company. Our insurance policy had a limit. The payout would be for the maximum amount covered. I knew the insurance would not pay for the total estimated cost of the damage. Third-party claims adjustors started knocking on my door. One after another offered to work on my behalf for only 5 percent of the total insurance proceeds. But what value were they providing?

I already knew what the insurance was going to pay, and they wanted me to hand them 5 percent of that total. I was supposed to choose one of them in the hope they could get the insurance to cover an amount above my policy limit. I leaned on common sense to provide a counter offer of 20 percent of any amount collected OVER the known payout. I made each one the same offer. Everyone got up and left because they knew they weren't really offering me anything.

After the tornado, I clearly explained to a contractor I would need a formal bid before hiring him. He ignored me, booked a private plane to Memphis and hired 50-day laborers to pick up debris at my facility. When he showed up on my property, he said I needed to learn to trust someone. I'd never met this man before the tornado and I now knew he was a thief and a fool. I instructed him to leave my property or be arrested for trespassing. I let him know it was the police I trusted. He sued me for $250,000. He messed with the wrong woman. It didn't take much common sense to know I would fight him. That's exactly what I did until he finally gave up.

At this point, the company was only operating as a non-alcoholic beverage facility. I hired a business expansion consultant to find a partner to fund the cost of restarting the brewery. At the time, I didn't want to sell the company. He sent me an engagement contract, which I read thoroughly. I always look for clauses that could possibly cause problems. As usual, they assumed I lacked education, experience and common sense. The consultant wanted to bind me to paying a commission on any prospect I might hire during our agreement and for twelve months after it ended.

Common sense told me they would claim everyone was a prospect. I changed the language requiring them to provide a final list of candidates on the termination date of the agreement. These were the only prospects who qualified for the 12-month extension. They forgot the language change after I sold the brewery. They received no payout. The buyer's name wasn't on the list they had provided.

Common sense and education have been handy with my family, too. My daughter had a car accident on her high school campus. The other student's parent was a teacher at the school. She called my husband and said Whitney hit her daughter's car because she was distracted by the loud music she played. She assumed my daughter was just a distracted teenager. I asked my daughter what happened. She said neither she or the other student looked as they backed up until the crash. I knew Whitney's explanation was honest. Why? Whitney was always bold enough to tell you what was on her mind. She would not allow a bad situation to compromise her integrity. Later, we learned an independent witness observed the accident. He only spoke with a school administrator. His account of the accident was exactly as my daughter described. The disappointment was this teacher used stereotyping in an attempt to win her case.

The next year, my son was in her advanced algebra class. The teacher knew he was Whitney's brother and she used her grading power to exert power over him. I removed him from her classroom and his stress went away and his grades returned to A's.

Common sense tells you that education will benefit you in life. But education won't always teach you common sense. It takes time to fine-tune that intuitive voice in your head. Remember, haste makes waste. Take a minute to think about the best course of action. Great leaders don't make snap decisions without their common sense and trust in what they have learned in life. Education doesn't just come from books, either. Seek mentors who you trust to test your judgment on select decisions. Becoming a great leader is a bit like rock climbing: Take your time, trust your instincts, educate yourself and don't forget to look up. It's the only way to reach the top.

X

Be Transparent

My mother didn't hide the truth of our circumstances from us. She didn't sugarcoat our situation. She made it clear her life wasn't the one she wished upon her children or anyone else. She used every success and failure in her life to teach her children right from wrong and good versus evil. She shared her life choices in a manner meant to make us better—not bitter. As a result, mom was transparent and trusted by everyone. "Transparency is the cousin of honesty" was based upon mom's life as our role model.

Not all parents are like that. Many of them hide what they experienced as teenagers. Those formidable years are when young people begin to gain their independence and test boundaries. Rather than sharing their own challenges, some parents pretend they were perfect. Instead of using their experiences to help their children make better choices, some hide financial difficulties, problems in their marriage or other relationships from their children. They want to protect them, but children are smart and resilient. They know when something is wrong. Pretending everything is OK often causes trust issues and problems between young people and their parents. Honesty breeds better relationships.

I have a great memory because I only have to remember one version of every story—the truth. Great leaders know the power in honesty, and they realize it's non-negotiable. The loss of trust is the ultimate violation in business or personal relationships.

The demise of trust may start with a white lie about a problem that often began with some rationalization. People use justifications, posturing or a slight twist of a fact as a substitution for the truth. In reality, these are the times when your ability to take a stance on honesty and trust is tested. Just tell the truth.

Truth is as vital to leadership as breath is to survival. You can't lead successfully on a mountain of lies.

People have to trust you. Great leaders know honesty is not just about integrity. It is about freedom, as well. You can sleep at night knowing nobody has the ability to take away your integrity. The only person who can give it up is you. There is power and comfort in knowing you control your honesty.

When I became a human resource manager, I gave everybody a clean slate. I told all the employees I was giving them blind trust. I believed what they said to me until they gave me a reason not to. It was important for them to understand their integrity with me was in their hands. They knew I would investigate any problems, and so it was best to be honest from the start. They understood the value in the respect I had for a trustworthy relationship. Most employees did everything they could to protect it.

Whenever I had a one-on-one meeting, I always wrote everything down. When they saw me taking notes, they knew I was paying attention. Whatever they said mattered. The truth is writing down what they said kept me organized. It also let them know they were being heard. And as long as they were telling the truth, I would listen.

Employees often addressed a concern involving another team member. During these sessions, I asked clarifying questions. Then I would review my notes with them to ensure I had the facts straight. When they realized I would be meeting with everyone named in their complaint, they would often request an urgent second meeting. After giving it some thought, they needed to explain the statement to protect their integrity.

Employees understood my expectations and character. I worked to be transparent. They knew I didn't just walk the walk. I did what I said and said what I did. They knew I would not play games with their careers.

I've always stressed the importance of honesty. Being dishonest is the fastest way to lose your integrity. Once it's gone, it's nearly impossible to get back. No situation is worth losing your integrity over. The truth is the truth—so stick to it.

When I was an HR manager, I always focused on the facts during grievance meetings. It sometimes placed individuals in a bad light. It didn't matter. I knew the truth would help us get to the root of the problem. We were more likely to find a swifter resolution if all the cards were laid on the table.

Employees started to see I wasn't controlled by emotions or influenced by someone's position. They came to understand I was interested in the best solution for everyone. In my entire career, I have never twisted the truth or sided with someone because of their title. In fact, my integrity helped the employees at Smucker's realize they didn't need the Teamsters union. Unions are necessary to level the playing field against managers who may lack integrity. When the union was being decertified, I educated each employee on their state and federal labor law rights without a union. I always let honesty be my guide.

Word will get around about your integrity. You'll either be known for having it—or not. Make sure it's not the latter. For example, an employee from another department once called me to report he was sick. I asked if he notified his manager. He said, "Yes, but he will lie and say I didn't call in." He would be terminated for job abandonment. I asked, "Why did you call me?" He said, "Everyone knows you always tell the truth." I reported the absence and documented the date, time and reason in an e-mail. Employees had reported instances of absenteeism not reported by management. I asked the manager about the concern. He said it wasn't true.

My son Chris was a cross-country runner. Training consisted of running outside for miles. The team wasn't monitored. Instead, they practiced on the honor system. His coach spoke with my husband one day, while the team completed a workout. He knew some of the team members took shortcuts. They believed he didn't know it. As a coach, he was required to actually make sure they completed their training. He said he couldn't ask Chris because everyone knew he always told the truth. So he asked someone else, who valued relationships over honesty. He didn't want to put our son on the spot in front of his teammates.

After assuming a new job as vice president, I learned that managers and employees lacked trust. As a result, they maintained an "us-versus-them" environment. This communications barrier destroyed the facility's efficiency and reputation. Therefore, I decided to use our safety program to build trust, which improved relationships. If a company does not handle safety concerns, the indirect message to employees is the company cares more about profits than people. Since our system tracked and prioritized safety work orders, I decided to make this information public. We posted all issues with the date, severity, planned corrective action and date resolved. The safety document was discussed at all team meetings. Any issue open past the target completion date was brought to my attention. We solicited employee input for creative ideas on corrective actions.

Amazingly, the lines of communications opened up for other topics. If employees could openly share safety concerns and recommendations, they could trust management with other topics. Employees don't care about your business if you do not care about them, which is their business. My leadership team learned transparency is the cousin of honesty.

Kirsten Gillibrand, an author and New York State Senator said, "I find that when you open the door towards openness and transparency, a lot of people will follow you through." Lead by example. Remember: You want to be the person you would like your children to be. Use your honesty to draw a line in the sand. Let others know what you stand for in any situation. The end result will be people in your personal and professional life will realize they need to conduct themselves with integrity if they want to have a healthy relationship with you. Honesty is the best policy, and transparency really is the cousin of honesty.

Become the Pro

My mother's definition of a pro applies to anyone or any situation. She taught us to find our gifts and maximize their potential by giving everything we had in that particular space. It doesn't matter if you are a garbage man, used car salesman or leader, be the best. It was her way of saying be the pro everyone admires and seeks for guidance. David Maister, a great writer and former Harvard professor, once said, "Professional is not a label you give yourself. It's a description you hope others will apply to you."

Great leaders motivate others to optimize performance. My mentor once told me my job as a plant manager wasn't to perform tasks but to get the best out of others. I was evaluated on my ability to maximize the potential and performance of 150 employees to create value for the company.

As leaders, we sometimes forget people are more complex than machines. They have emotions and the world comes at them from many different directions. Leaders must remain professional at all times. Additionally, a leader must be objective when dealing with others.

A manager once said to me, "Employees don't think managers have problems." I responded, "They know you have problems, but it is not their job to deal with your problems. It's your job to deal with their problems. If their emotional state is out of control, it impacts the company's performance."

When I was 20 years old, the plant manager's style of management was to shout and then ask questions. He was such a screamer that I would only deliver bad news to him after 5 p.m. It enabled me to prepare for the emotional attack and no one would hear him screaming because the office was closed. Even in adverse situations, I learned. I knew from my mom that you catch more flies with honey. This guy wasn't catching flies, and he certainly wasn't developing relationships.

As a new manager, I would have group conversations to avoid speaking with individuals. When I needed to correct the behavior of a single employee, I called a meeting with my entire department. I didn't think I was wrong until a subordinate old enough to be my mother requested a meeting. In the meeting, she told me I was wasting her time by calling a group meeting. I needed to speak directly to the person with the issue. Without being rude, she was direct and to the point.

This advice has influenced my counseling style for over 30 years. I learned to deliver bad news in person rather than hide behind a phone, e-mail, text or crowd. This was my first introduction to "managing up." This term refers to a subordinate providing guidance and advice to a superior. Many times throughout my career, I've found it incredibly helpful. But it's important to be respectful when you are managing up.

I had a superior who was a micromanager. If I went on vacation, he would make decisions in my absence based upon limited information or poor assumptions. The first time it happened, I felt he undermined my authority, which made me angry. The next vacation, I instructed my team to contact me if he called. My team would provide a written response to his inquiry, detailing corrective actions that were in process. They didn't leave anything open-ended since he would fill in the blank. It prevented him from making decisions that negatively impacted our facility. The written recommendations prepared him for corporate meetings regarding my facility. He was the boss and I had to be creative to control the boss. By being creative, he maintained his power while I maintained control of my facility. All successful leaders manage up.

Becoming the pro enabled me to make the most significant leadership decision of my life. The journey began in February 2001. As the vice president of Memphis operations, I was hired to make drastic improvements at Coors. Our facility had the highest costs and the poorest safety record. To make matters worse, the quality of the product was lacking and the team's reputation was in the gutter. It took two years to turn the plant around.

We cut costs by $20 million and improved performance in all categories. Unfortunately, there are no guarantees in life. The company decided to shut down the facility.

After the closing announcement, I evaluated my options for my next career move. I dreamed of buying the plant myself. But the initial asking price was $40 million. With so much work to do, I had to put those aspirations aside.

As plant manager and vice president, it was my job to develop strategies to keep employees focused. During this time, I entertained potential buyers, which excited the staff because it gave them hope. During the tours, I listened to prospective buyers discuss the "potential business" at the site. What interested me was their ideas were consistent with the "what if" games I was playing about buying the facility myself.

A few weeks later, my confidence to pursue the acquisition became stronger. I attended a meeting with the vice president of the local chamber. He inquired about the status of the brewery sale. I told him there was one outside bidder, but I would like to make the purchase.

That same week, I was asked by Coors to consider a transfer to Shenandoah, to manage the startup of the new brewery. They also asked what job within Coors would make me happy professionally. They wanted an answer by Monday. That same day, I discovered the price had dropped to one-third of the original price. It was time to leave an impression.

The weekend before the meeting, I had trouble sleeping. My mind raced with possibilities. As with everything, I shared my desire to start a business with my mother. She said with my drive, determination and experience, I had what it took to do anything. I was excited one minute and scared the next. I was confident I could be successful but nervous because women don't always receive equal opportunities.

Monday morning, I met with the COO of Coors. I said, "First I need you to take me seriously." He agreed, and I told him I wanted to submit a bid to purchase the brewery. You could have heard a pin drop on the other end of the phone. He didn't believe I could raise the capital. He felt it was only a matter of time before I would walk away. Even with all my hard work, I had not impressed him enough as a woman to be considered a possible buyer. It was about to change.

The day came when I walked into a room with six prestigious white males, who bid on the brewery where I worked. These men were CEOs and lawyers. They were strong and confident. It impressed me but it didn't intimidate me. I was David and they were my Goliaths. Society said I should not be at that table. But there I sat exuding my own air of confidence. They looked for any flicker of weakness, but I left the impression I was there to play. I wasn't going away. I spent eight months on the deal. It was an emotional roller coaster. It was exciting one minute; frustrating and intimidating the next. I mentally cataloged the negative situations as strategies to get me to quit. I became more determined. What was eye-opening was some of those who should have supported me didn't. However, those who did encourage me were a refreshing surprise.

Against all the odds, Hardy Bottling Company was born. I stepped out of my role as an employee and became the founder of my own company. The journey to get there was long and arduous, but worth every struggle for every triumph.

For me, becoming the pro meant becoming the owner. It may mean something entirely different for you. You must take steps to learn all you can. Always look up to see what opportunities are just out of your grasp. Then, reach out and grab them. Make it happen. Become the pro.

X

Keep Calm and Carry On

It was Super Tuesday and states across the country were holding primary elections. For me and over 100 people I worked with, it was merely business as usual. The only thing special about that morning and afternoon was I had several clients in from out of town to run tests.

Coors made modifications at my facility to produce their product. They had worked on the project for more than three months. They were pleased with the progress. It was Feb. 5 and we planned a test run of their products in March. They were almost finished. We weren't prepared for what happened next. There were certainly modifications made that day. They just weren't the ones we expected.

One of our other client's, Republic Tea, was there for a plant trial. They are a gourmet tea company sold in white tablecloth restaurants.

All the clients were in the plant, while I met with a few managers in my office. When we started the meeting, the skies outside my window were clear. We were engrossed in our discussion, so no one noticed the change in the weather until there was a hard knock at my door. It was Phil Potts, my director of maintenance. He told us to get to the basement at once. There was a tornado heading straight towards us. Everyone else was running for safety. I stood up and looked out the window. It was pitch black outside. We had safety procedures in place and everybody followed the plan. The procedures were the same from the days when Coors owned the plant.

As soon as we got in the basement, the tornado hit. We could hear the building being torn apart. Employees outside tried to get into the shelter, but the wind pressure would not allow the doors to open. Everything happened so fast. It was just a matter of seconds. The noise was terrible, and I just knew the plant was being demolished by the tornado.

When we emerged, my greatest concern was to ensure no one was hurt. It was hard to ignore the destruction as I went in search of everyone. I was incredibly grateful no one was injured.

The employees in the warehouse jumped in the pit beneath the trains. It was a miracle the trains were there that day. The tornado blew off the 30 feet high steel doors, which would have landed on top of employees if not for the trains. Production and brewing employees all went to the cellar.

We had truck drivers, who slept in their rigs on the property. One of them slept through the entire tornado. There were three men who worked the gates. They all crammed into a single toilet stall in the corner of a tiny 10-by-10 office. The space was barely big enough for one person, but it kept them safe. There wasn't a single person with even a scratch. It was a miracle.

The clients from out of town were terrified. When they came in, they were visibly shaken. After we confirmed there were no injuries, I started to assess the damage. It was clear the modifications Coors made were severely damaged. The air conditioning units weighed several tons and they were blown off the roof of the building. Walls were gone, and the roof had crumbled. It was a major hit.

I stood there looking at my life's work. Just 25 minutes earlier, the building was fine. I knew everyone would look to me for guidance. I had to be their lighthouse, and I needed to stay calm. I would also need to develop a plan to rebuild and get the company operational as soon as possible. There was no time to waste.

I peeked in the plant and saw there was water everywhere. I had to leave the building because the risk of electrocution was too great.

Two different power grids serviced the brewery. During the previous five years, the facility never lost power. If one grid went down, the other one came online. This tornado took both grids out and we lost all power. It was off for over two weeks.

That night, we shut the gas off to the property. Next, we had to hire armed security to patrol the facility. Then, I needed some sleep in order to face the next day.

When I got home that night, I felt like the weight of the world was on my shoulders. My children and husband were waiting for me. It was one night they were not going to bed. My children asked me an interesting question, "Mom, why would God do this when you work so hard?" I thought for a moment and said, "Let me get some sleep. I have to be at the plant as soon as the sun comes up. I want to thank you for staying up. I'm going to be OK. I'll try to figure it out but not tonight." I wanted to leave them with the assurance I wasn't defeated. I needed to answer their question about God, so I offered this, "I don't know what God is saying. I wish I did. But I'm not willing to say He is saying anything bad. Let's give it some time." Then, I sent them off to bed.

It took until Friday to give them an honest answer. I knew then God had done me a favor. I had run the numbers to figure out how to make the insurance work in my favor. I called my mother and told her the tornado was actually a blessing from God. She said, "If you believe it, then I believe it." The insurance enabled me to repair the facility and make it even better than before.

To overcome hardship, I had to keep calm. I had to look at the circumstances I had been dealt and figure out how to succeed. I couldn't change the fact a tornado had ripped through my building. I couldn't get back the clients who decided to leave. I had no control over my circumstances. None of it was my fault but fixing it was my responsibility.

Leadership opportunities often show up through the toughest of circumstances. The phrase, "Keep calm and carry on," was first used in promotional posters during World War II, when bombs were falling all over the place. They were printed by the British government in the hopes of encouraging the people to carry on with their lives as normal. Surprisingly, it's precisely what they did. Malcolm Gladwell talks about it in his book David and Goliath. He said each time a bomb dropped, all the people who survived were actually motivated. They had faced their worst fears and made it out alive. In fact, they were often elated.

When you're faced with a challenge, you must keep calm and find a solution. It will be better if you make it a lesson or develop a strategy to work it in your favor. Success in a storm or any turmoil requires planning, perseverance and a "can-do" attitude.

The insurance representative said a tornado of that magnitude would have destroyed a typical client. Instead, I chose to find strength in the circumstances. These were incredibly hard times, so don't be fooled.

Sometimes life and your sense of normal must break in order to have a breakthrough. In the end, the outcome is a matter of choice.

Michelle Obama said, "You may not always have a comfortable life. And you'll not always be able to solve all of the world's problems at once. But don't ever underestimate the impact you can have, because history has shown us courage can be contagious, and hope can take on a life of its own."

To lead, you have to set an example. People will look to you for guidance. Seize the opportunity. When the plant was hit, I had a team that counted on me for a paycheck. They needed me to be their rock and find solutions so they could feed their families. In the end, I was able to give them more than just a paycheck. I gave them hope that it would not only be OK but would also be better for everyone. I seized the moment rather than letting the moment seize me.

Remember, the storms will always hit. But when they do, don't quit. The power of the mind is mightier than any storm. Keep calm and carry on, indeed. It's the only way to succeed as a true leader.

X

Be Prepared

Life often comes at you sideways when you least expect it. The only thing you can plan for 100 percent of the time is that you can't plan for everything. Great leaders know you must be prepared for the unexpected.

After going through everything related to buying the brewery, I was finally able to call myself the owner. My first company was a multimillion-dollar bottling facility, and the buck stopped with me.

I no longer had a home office to call when there was a problem. My office was the home office. So when I got the call from my doctor just two weeks after I completed the purchase of the plant from Coors, I was caught off guard.

I was at the hairdresser when I received the call. It was after five p.m. which was unusual. The doctor got right to the point and said, "Carolyn, I have bad news. Your mammogram came back showing a lump."

I didn't react because I was in shock. My mind was reeling. I had invested 50 percent of the family's wealth in this company. I had two children who were at home and planning to go to college. My family could not operate this business without me. It was my vision, experience and business plan we were executing.

In my mind I screamed, *What have I gotten the family into? If I do not recover, they will suffer because of my ambitions.* The only thing I knew to do was get prepared. My doctor said there was no way to know the severity without a biopsy. But she also said, "Carolyn, I need to you to take this seriously and make this procedure a priority."

Even though there was no way of knowing the outcome she didn't want to wait to find out. She said, "I know you are under a lot of pressure with your new company but this situation is more than a distraction." We scheduled the biopsy right away, and I waited weeks for my answer.

The first week, I was in survival mode. I had put together a management team from people I worked with in the past. But they weren't supposed to start until January. I asked them to begin working immediately. These two managers were my trusted allies and confidants. They had my back. When I shared my diagnosis with them in confidence, they each gave their two-week notices and came on board.

Three weeks later, I got the results no one wants to hear. It was cancer. The next month, I had a lumpectomy. Unfortunately, cancer had spread and the lumpectomy wasn't effective. We had to take the next step. It was clear I needed a mastectomy to have the best chance of beating the disease. The mastectomy was performed the week before Thanksgiving.

The next month, I had a port catheter placed in my chest for chemotherapy. After one month, the catheter came out and I was back in surgery. I had surgery every month from October through January. I did all of it while trying to get my new startup company off the ground. I did what I had to do to be prepared.

During this time, I kept thinking, God didn't bring me this far to die. I kept a positive attitude. Initially, I didn't share my battle with my siblings. My family was always my chief concern. At work, my cancer was never discussed because I was terrified lenders would call in the loan.

I battled cancer and won. I have the scars to prove it! I wouldn't wish that time on anyone, but it made me a stronger person both physically and emotionally.

Being prepared means being strategic. No matter what comes your way. Preparation comes from building a great support team, keeping a calm head and building a strategy. You have to be ready for anything. It works both professionally and personally!

Another aspect of being prepared is doing your homework. When you negotiate anything, be sure you know as much about the subject matter as you can. It may be necessary to bring in professionals, like an attorney, to look over a contract before signing it. It could mean researching your company's needs before asking for a promotion. Or it could mean communicating thoroughly in writing before entering into a partnership.

My mom always said the dating period is the honeymoon. It's when everybody is putting the best versions of themselves forward. Once you get married, you meet the everyday version of your significant other. That's when things get real.

It's similar in business. Partnerships go south because personalities clash. Partner A accuses partner B of not working as hard. Partner B thought they were just supposed to put money into the company. Start with the end in mind. What result do you want? Be bold by asking and knowing the facts. Then, get the deal in writing. We are human and we forget. Don't leave important details or conversations in your head. When there is a disagreement, you'll be prepared because you have a contract. Ensure everybody is on the same page by summarizing verbal conversations with a written account.

As you succeed, you'll find lots of people come to you for help. They may want your time or your money. Be prepared for both requests. I make it a policy to have a plan for these types of requests. Time is a precious commodity. I support organizations and non-profits who have missions that are aligned with my own. I encourage you to say no to requests that don't align with your personal interests, passions or skills.

When people ask to borrow money, you have to have a plan or it gets complicated. Otherwise, you start receiving lots of requests. My heart always goes out to the NBA, NFL or any professional player who comes into a lot of money. Many times, their families and friends think they won the lottery. The player is not ready for the emotional pleas. Perhaps an old friend wants to start a business and just needs a little upfront money. The player's conscience asks him, *How can a wealthy NBA player not help a childhood friend achieve his dreams?* In addition, young professionals (or overnight millionaires) don't have the experience to evaluate whether a business plan or individual is bankable. They often end up losing the money, and the relationship is damaged. The family member or friend avoids them because they feel guilty for failing to repay the loan. As you become successful, it's better to say no to these types of requests. If the relationship is strong, they will get over the no.

When you loan money to people, they never go away. You don't have to be wealthy for the requests to start pouring in. I'm sure most people have a family member who is always in need of help.

I have relatives who create great hard-luck stories. They need shoes for their child or medication for their baby. Perhaps, the boss treated them poorly. My first rule is the child will get medication and shoes. My second rule is you have to work for it.

I always have something that needs to be done and I don't give loans. I once received a phone call from a father, who needed shoes for his child. I asked how much he needed and he gave me a number. I told him I needed a hole dug for the installation of new electrical service. He did the work and I paid him for it. He didn't owe me anything when he was done. There was no guilt or remorse on his part. It's always better to give the prospective borrower work, which allows them to maintain their dignity and be debt-free. The next time they need something, they are prepared to work for it. You would be amazed at how many people stop asking for money when they understand this policy of mine. I'm always prepared for these situations.

Finally, it's important to be the most-prepared person in the room. If you are going to a meeting, research the people who will be in attendance. What makes them tick? How long have they been in business? What interests them? Find out everything you can about them and their company.

Today's technology makes it easy to research people and their backgrounds. You might not be able to use
the information you find, but it will help you see them
as human. When it comes time to present or negotiate,
you'll have a connection to them.

Leaders try to stay one step ahead of everyone else.
It's the only way they can lead. Educating yourself and
plan ahead. Arm yourself with information and you will
find preparation will be a byproduct of your work.

Lead by Example

Too many people think leadership qualities are reserved for extraordinary people. But we all have a leader inside of us. Some of us display leadership qualities in our personal lives as parents, siblings or friends. Others demonstrate the same qualities at work or in the community. But the one constant in great leaders is they lead by example. If you want to bring out the greatness in others, you have to show them what greatness looks like. If you want them to be courageous, you must have courage too.

There is an old story about a mother in India, who was concerned about her son eating too much sugar. She took him to see Mahatma Gandhi. She asked Gandhi to tell her son to stop eating too much sugar and inform him it wasn't good for him. Gandhi looked at her and said, "No. Bring him back to me in two weeks and I will speak to him." So she did. When she returned with her son, Gandhi told the young boy, "Stop eating too much sugar. It's bad for you." The mother was confused. "Why didn't you just tell him two weeks ago when I asked you to the first time?" asked the mother. "Because two weeks ago, I was eating too much sugar myself," he said. And so it goes. You shouldn't ask others to do that which you are not willing to do yourself. You must lead by example.

I was 32-years-old when I was promoted to quality manager. When the announcement was made, one employee made a loud gasp, while others stared in shock. Let's just say I wasn't the popular choice.

The staff had been living on easy street since their previous manager was extremely laid back. He rarely followed up after giving assignments. And he never held anyone accountable. As a result, the entire team had a history of poor performance, poor attendance and low morale. Out of the company's 13 locations, our plant was dead last. The quality team lacked respect because policy compliance was virtually non-existent.

So, there I was—the new manager. I had a reputation for running a tight ship. I'm detail-oriented, I hold my teams accountable, and I inspect what I expect. That was a major change for the team, but I didn't want to lose them. They understood the policies and procedures that would lead to success. The problem was a lack of support from upper management and they followed management's example.

This team rose to the level of their leadership, but they deserved a chance to shine. They needed guidance and accountability. We all do. I had a job to do, which was to lead each of them to achieve their personal best and to become the number-one team.

The team needed a boost to their confidence and a few short-term, low-hanging wins. I used my analytical skills to assess the easiest problems to fix and got to work. The internal audit reports were shared with the staff. I validated the discrepancy to ensure we dealt with a real issue. It demonstrated I had their back.

When there were concerns mentioned on any of the quality reports, I always asked team members for their opinions. The end result was ownership of changes and buy-in that supported the modifications of procedures.

The change required department managers to develop solutions and implement corrective actions before the next audit.

When the following week's audit was performed, most issues were addressed. It surprised and energized the team. Moving forward, every issue became an opportunity to work together. The team's accomplishments improved everyone's self-esteem and gave them sense of purpose. Eventually, the hard work paid off.

The team with the worst attendance record, no respect and no sense of urgency went from the last place to the top performer in the entire company. They even had the best attendance record! Even better, our location received an "Excellent" audit score—the first in the company's history—for doing such a great job.

How did it happen? You first have to set the example. Next, you have to set the expectation. And then, you have to hold people accountable to the expectation. When there is a problem, you include those involved in the creation of the solution. Finally, you give them the tools they need to succeed.

A great leader meets people where they are. They take the time to get to know others. It helps to be aware of the strengths and weaknesses of those you lead. Everyone has unique talents and abilities. Make sure you harvest those gifts in the people you lead.

I had one employee who was responsible, dependable and paid considerable attention to detail. She had the traits that are hard to teach. However, her confidence was at an all-time low because she wasn't adequately trained. We had a one-size-fits-all training process and it just doesn't work. People learn in different ways. It's the responsibility of the leader to ensure the message and the instruction are received and understood.

When we gave her the proper tools and training, she felt valued and respected. By taking the time to train her properly, we demonstrated to the entire team they were appreciated by the company. We cared enough to find creative ways to assist with their success.

Great sports teams are made up of athletes who each bring their own unique sets of skills. Not everyone is a quarterback or point guard. The coach's goal is to maximize each player's talents individually to improve performance of the entire team.

Leaders understand that successful companies build great teams. Successful families make great teams. Pay attention to the skills of those you lead. It may be your children, or it may be your staff. Celebrate their unique differences and foster their talents. In the end, everybody wins.

Always Pursue Growth

If we compare growth to scaling a mountain, there are three different types of climbers. For all three, the objective is the same: reach the top. After all, everyone raves about the summit. The view from the top is breathtaking. We imagine taking that final step as we arrive. We see ourselves putting the flag in the ground, as we declare our victory with great pride.

Imagine each climber's backpack loaded with all the essentials needed to make the ascent. Many of the tools are the same for each person. Yet, each of them has packed at least one additional tool that's a bit different from the others.

One climber packed fear, one packed unworthiness and one packed faith. The actions of the first climber are predominantly molded by fear--of the unknown, of the sheer height of the mountain and of failure. All of the "what-ifs" begin to play like a broken record in that climber's mind. Sometimes, this climber no more begins the ascent before they end up retreating back to the beginning. Sometimes, they never even take a single step forward.

This first climber resembles those who are stuck in life. They have accepted their lot—no matter how unfortunate it seems. They don't pursue growth because it's too painful and too scary to step into the unknown. To grow requires you to step outside of your comfort zone. This climber is just too comfortable with what he can count on and what he knows—even when it is misery. Unhappiness is his comfort.

The renowned psychologist Abraham Maslow once said, "One can choose to go backward toward safety or forward toward growth. Growth must be chosen again and again. Fear must be overcome again and again."

Many people wish to reach the top of the mountain. But few have the desire to do the work to scale it. It's much easier to stay within the status quo. It's far more common for people to accept what life dishes out than to demand more and go after it. Climbing to the summit is hard work.

Unlike the first climber, the second one, who packed unworthiness, is quick to begin his climb. He ascends with a sort of desperate pace and rushes to get to the top. He is often callous and careless in his mad pursuit of victory.

This climber resembles those who burden themselves with more work than what's healthy. They spend most of their days plotting, working and stressing. They live on a crazed hamster wheel that never stops. They must work harder, do more, acquire more and be more. For this climber, enough is never enough.

Their effort to reach the summit is their attempt to finally feel the worthiness that seems to always be just one step away. It's elusive because they never understand what they're reaching for is something they had all along. This climber never slows down long enough to learn the real lessons leading to personal growth and true fulfillment.

The third climber is tapped into their inner GPS. They understand personal growth is not about acquiring material things. It's about pursuing the path your creator intended for you to walk. It requires you to pack your faith. It's what the third climber uses to ascend the mountain. This person doesn't rush the journey. They realize their ascension up the mountain also provides valuable lessons, which enable them to sustain the challenging heights.

My entire life, I watched my mother climb mountains. I know there were times when, like the first climber, she must have been afraid. She climbed anyway. Each hardship she overcame became a building block for her children. Each time she slipped, we watched her pick herself back up and continue the climb. We saw her fear turn to faith. Her faith ultimately turned into a strength, which fueled our dreams.

The one constant from my mother was her insistence for each of her children to challenge themselves. In the challenge is where the growth occurs.

Like my mother, the third climber leads by example. When they reach the summit, they know there are other mountains to climb, other lessons to learn and more growth to pursue. They start a new journey and look up at the prize from a new perspective. They understand the path will be tough and, at times, it will be lonely. But the journey will be worth it. For, in the end, reaching the top is not the end of the journey but the beginning of a new one.

X

Acknowledgments

This book has been a labor of love. My life started in such poverty that the only way to go was "Up." I was blessed to have great parents, Lois and Sidney Chism. My elegant, classy mom was a visionary who taught her children that your only limitation is you. She taught us selfless leadership and inspired us to learn continually. Mom, you are my "shero." Thank you for passing the baton of excellence and ambition. You made my life's work and this book possible because of your wisdom and your passion for education.

Any significant accomplishments in life require great partners. My greatest partner, soulmate, and spouse, Marino Hardy, has shown enduring respect and steadfast support of my journey. When we met as teenagers, he realized I was unique, and it didn't frighten him. Instead of being scared away, he signed up for a lifetime of change and challenges. My other great partners are our wonderful children: Jennifer, Whitney and Christopher. Thank you for your love, friendship and support of my endless pursuit of a different future. As children, they assumed what I did was normal. They now know my goal was to create a better world for them. They are thoughtful, driven and amazingly successful adults. They become number-one at anything they touch.

As the seventh of 16 children, my siblings were my village. They invested mentally, emotionally and financially in my accomplishments. My supportive brothers and sisters cultivated greatness in me at an early age. They sacrificed personally for my college education. Thank you for your love, support and guidance.

In life, everyone is looking for a break. Everyone wants someone to give them a chance. This thank you goes to my Smucker's family, who were insightful and courageous to see brilliance in a 20-year-old. They supported me as I blossomed from a shy, young accountant to a confident plant manager.

A special thank you to Staley Cates. While many were safely defining their position on inclusion, he chose to challenge the status quo.

I also want to say thank you to all the members of my loyal leadership teams. They were great supporters and champions, allowing us to grow together.

There are so many people who helped me get to where I am—too many to name here in these pages. I will be eternally grateful to all of you for sharing the heavy lifting by always encouraging me to "Look Up."